Amazon EC2 Cookbook

Over 40 hands-on recipes to develop and deploy
real-world applications using Amazon EC2

Sekhar Reddy

Aurobindo Sarkar

[PACKT] enterprise
PUBLISHING   professional expertise distilled

BIRMINGHAM - MUMBAI

Amazon EC2 Cookbook

First published: November 2015

Production reference: 1241115

Published by Packt Publishing Ltd.
Livery Place
35 Livery Street
Birmingham B3 2PB, UK.

ISBN 978-1-78528-004-7

www.packtpub.com

Credits

Authors

Sekhar Reddy

Aurobindo Sarkar

Reviewer

Mark Takacs

Commissioning Editor

Amarabha Banerjee

Acquisition Editor

Larissa Pinto

Content Development Editor

Athira Laji

Technical Editor

Prajakta Mhatre

Copy Editor

Charlotte Carneiro

Project Coordinator

Bijal Patel

Proofreader

Safis Editing

Indexer

Rekha Nair

Production Coordinator

Manu Joseph

Cover Work

Manu Joseph

About the Authors

Sekhar Reddy is a technology generalist. He has deep expertise in Windows, Unix, Linux OS, and programming languages, such as Java, C# , and Python.

Sekhar possesses 8 years of experience in designing large-scale systems/pipelines using REST, cloud technologies, NoSQL, relational databases, and big data technologies.

He enjoys new ways of solving difficult problems and brings the same kind of enthusiasm to design and code. He loves implementing innovative ideas, working on exciting products, and writing efficient code.

His current interests include IoT platforms, distributed systems, cloud computing, big data technologies, and web-scale applications.

Sekhar is working with a high-end technology consulting company, Mactores Innovations, as a senior research engineer, and has a MS in computer science from Kakatiya University.

Aurobindo Sarkar is actively working with several start-ups in the role of CTO/technical director. With a career spanning more than 22 years, he has consulted at some of the leading organizations in the the US, the UK, and Canada. He specializes in software-as-a-service product development, cloud computing, big data analytics, and machine learning. His domain expertise is in financial services, media, public sector, mobile gaming, and automotive sectors. Aurobindo has been actively working with technology startups for over 5 years now. As a member of the top leadership team at various startups, he has mentored several founders and CxOs, provided technology advisory services, developed cloud strategy, product roadmaps, and set up large engineering teams. Aurobindo has an MS (computer science) from New York University, M.Tech (management) from Indian Institute of Science, and B.Tech (engineering) from IIT Delhi.

About the Reviewer

Mark Takacs got his first job in the early 90s as the only applicant with HTML experience. Since then, his road to DevOps has spanned the traditional MVC software development on LAMP and Java, the front-end web development in JavaScript, HTML, CSS, network administration, build and release engineering, production operations, and a large helping of system administration throughout. Mark currently lives and works in Silicon Valley.

www.PacktPub.com

Support files, eBooks, discount offers, and more

For support files and downloads related to your book, please visit www.PacktPub.com.

Did you know that Packt offers eBook versions of every book published, with PDF and ePub files available? You can upgrade to the eBook version at www.PacktPub.com and as a print book customer, you are entitled to a discount on the eBook copy. Get in touch with us at service@packtpub.com for more details.

At www.PacktPub.com, you can also read a collection of free technical articles, sign up for a range of free newsletters and receive exclusive discounts and offers on Packt books and eBooks.

https://www2.packtpub.com/books/subscription/packtlib

Do you need instant solutions to your IT questions? PacktLib is Packt's online digital book library. Here, you can search, access, and read Packt's entire library of books.

Why subscribe?

► Fully searchable across every book published by Packt

► Copy and paste, print, and bookmark content

► On demand and accessible via a web browser

Free access for Packt account holders

If you have an account with Packt at www.PacktPub.com, you can use this to access PacktLib today and view 9 entirely free books. Simply use your login credentials for immediate access.

Instant updates on new Packt books

Get notified! Find out when new books are published by following @PacktEnterprise on Twitter or the *Packt Enterprise* Facebook page.

Table of Contents

Preface

With the increasing interest in leveraging cloud infrastructure around the world, AWS Cloud from Amazon offers a cutting-edge platform to architecture, build, and deploy web-scale cloud applications. The variety of services and features available from AWS can reduce the overall infrastructure costs and accelerate the development process for both large enterprises and startups alike. In such an environment, it is imperative for developers to be able to set up the required infrastructure and effectively use various cloud services provided by AWS. In addition, they also should be able to effectively secure access to their production environments and deploy and monitor their applications.

Amazon EC2 Cookbook will serve as a handy reference to developers building production applications or cloud-based products. It will be a trusted desktop reference book that you reach out to first, or refer to often, to find solutions to specific AWS development-related requirements and issues. If you have a specific task to be completed, then we expect you to jump straight to the appropriate recipe in the book. By working through the steps in a specific recipe, you can quickly accomplish the typical tasks and issues related to the infrastructure, development, and deployment of an enterprise-grade AWS Cloud application.

What this book covers

Chapter 1, Selecting and Configuring Amazon EC2 Instances, provides recipes to choose and configure the right EC2 instances to meet your application-specific requirements.

Chapter 2, Configuring and Securing a Virtual Private Cloud, contains networking-related recipes to configure and secure a virtual private cloud (VPC).

Chapter 3, Managing AWS Resources Using AWS CloudFormation, provides recipes to create and manage related AWS resources in an orderly manner.

Chapter 4, Securing Access to Amazon EC2 Instances, deals with recipes for using the AWS Identity and Access Management (IAM) service to secure access to your Amazon EC2 instances.

Chapter 5, Monitoring Amazon EC2 Instances, contains recipes for monitoring your EC2 instances using AWS CloudWatch. It will also cover a related topic—autoscaling.

Chapter 6, Using AWS Data Services, contains recipes for using various AWS relational and NoSQL data services in AWS applications.

Chapter 7, Accessing Other AWS Services, contains recipes for accessing key AWS services (other than AWS data services). These services include Route 53, Amazon S3, AWS SES, AWS SNS, and AWS SQS.

Chapter 8, Deploying AWS Applications, talks about the recipes for AWS application deployments using Docker containers, Chef cookbooks, and Puppet recipes.

What you need for this book

You will need a standard development machine and an Amazon account to execute the recipes in this book.

Who this book is for

This book is targeted at advanced programmers, who have prior exposure to AWS concepts and features. The reader is likely to have built small applications and/or created some proof-of-concept applications. We are targeting developers tasked with building more complex applications or cloud-based products in startup or enterprise settings.

Sections

In this book, you will find several headings that appear frequently (Getting ready, How to do it, How it works, There's more, and See also).

To give clear instructions on how to complete a recipe, we use these sections as follows:

Getting ready

This section tells you what to expect in the recipe and describes how to set up any software or any preliminary settings required for the recipe.

How to do it...

This section contains the steps required to follow the recipe.

How it works...

This section usually consists of a detailed explanation of what happened in the previous section.

There's more...

This section consists of additional information about the recipe in order to make the reader more knowledgeable about the recipe.

See also

This section provides helpful links to other useful information for the recipe.

Conventions

In this book, you will find a number of text styles that distinguish between different kinds of information. Here are some examples of these styles and an explanation of their meaning.

Code words in text, database table names, folder names, filenames, file extensions, pathnames, dummy URLs, user input, and Twitter handles are shown as follows:
"If Python is already installed on your machine, then skip to the pip installation step."

A block of code is set as follows:

```
<dependency>
    <groupId>com.amazonaws</groupId>
    <artifactId>aws-java-sdk</artifactId>
    <version>1.9.28.1</version>
</dependency>
```

Any command-line input or output is written as follows:

```
$ aws ec2 authorize-security-group-ingress
--group-id sg-f332ea96
--protocol tcp
--port 11211
--cidr 0.0.0.0/0
```

New terms and **important words** are shown in bold. Words that you see on the screen, for example, in menus or dialog boxes, appear in the text like this: "Choose **Columns** for more details."

Warnings or important notes appear in a box like this.

Tips and tricks appear like this.

Reader feedback

Feedback from our readers is always welcome. Let us know what you think about this book—what you liked or disliked. Reader feedback is important for us as it helps us develop titles that you will really get the most out of.

To send us general feedback, simply e-mail feedback@packtpub.com, and mention the book's title in the subject of your message.

If there is a topic that you have expertise in and you are interested in either writing or contributing to a book, see our author guide at www.packtpub.com/authors.

Customer support

Now that you are the proud owner of a Packt book, we have a number of things to help you to get the most from your purchase.

Downloading the example code

You can download the example code files from your account at http://www.packtpub.com for all the Packt Publishing books you have purchased. If you purchased this book elsewhere, you can visit http://www.packtpub.com/support and register to have the files e-mailed directly to you.

Errata

Although we have taken every care to ensure the accuracy of our content, mistakes do happen. If you find a mistake in one of our books—maybe a mistake in the text or the code—we would be grateful if you could report this to us. By doing so, you can save other readers from frustration and help us improve subsequent versions of this book. If you find any errata, please report them by visiting http://www.packtpub.com/submit-errata, selecting your book, clicking on the **Errata Submission Form** link, and entering the details of your errata. Once your errata are verified, your submission will be accepted and the errata will be uploaded to our website or added to any list of existing errata under the Errata section of that title.

To view the previously submitted errata, go to `https://www.packtpub.com/books/content/support` and enter the name of the book in the search field. The required information will appear under the **Errata** section.

Piracy

Piracy of copyrighted material on the Internet is an ongoing problem across all media. At Packt, we take the protection of our copyright and licenses very seriously. If you come across any illegal copies of our works in any form on the Internet, please provide us with the location address or website name immediately so that we can pursue a remedy.

Please contact us at `copyright@packtpub.com` with a link to the suspected pirated material.

We appreciate your help in protecting our authors and our ability to bring you valuable content.

Questions

If you have a problem with any aspect of this book, you can contact us at `questions@packtpub.com`, and we will do our best to address the problem.

1
Selecting and Configuring Amazon EC2 Instances

In this chapter, we will cover recipes for:

- ▶ Choosing the right AWS EC2 instance types
- ▶ Preparing AWS CLI tools
- ▶ Launching EC2 instances using EC2-Classic and EC2-VPC
- ▶ Allocating Elastic IP addresses
- ▶ Creating an instance with multiple NIC cards and a static private IP address
- ▶ Selecting the right storage for your EC2 instance
- ▶ Creating tags for consistency
- ▶ Configuring security groups
- ▶ Creating an EC2 key pair
- ▶ Grouping EC2 instances using placement groups
- ▶ Configuring Elastic Load Balancing
- ▶ Architecting for high availability
- ▶ Creating instances for AWS Marketplace

Introduction

You need to ask yourself several questions in order to choose the right AWS EC2 instance for meeting your requirements. These include: What is the primary purpose of the EC2 instance being provisioned? What is the duration of your need for a particular machine? Do you need high performance storage? Should you go for dedicated or shared tenancy? Will the machine be used for compute-intensive or memory-intensive processing? What are the scalability, availability, and security requirements? What are your networking requirements? There are several options available for each of these parameters, and we will describe them in our recipes for making the right choices. For low latency, you can host your application in the AWS region nearest to the end user. Each AWS region is a separate geographic area, and has multiple isolated locations called availability zones. These availability zones are individual data centers in each region. They are used to deploy fault-tolerant and highly available applications. The latency between these availability zones is very low. If something goes wrong in an availability zone, then it does not affect the systems in another availability zone.

Choosing the right AWS EC2 instance types

An EC2 instance is a virtual machine hosted on the AWS Cloud. As an instance creator, you have root privileges on any instances you started. An EC2 instance can be used to host one or more of web servers, application servers, database servers, or backend processes/services requiring heavy compute or graphics processing. Depending on your application architecture, you can choose to host various components distributed across multiple EC2 instances.

AWS offers different types of storage attachments viz. SSD and magnetic. If you require higher storage performance, then ensure that the EC2 instance type you choose supports SSD.

There are three distinct purchasing options available for provisioning the AWS EC2 instances:

  ▶ **On-demand instances**: These instances are billed on an hourly basis and no upfront payments are required. Applications with unpredictable workloads or short-duration requirements are best handled using on-demand instances. This is the default purchasing option in AWS.

  ▶ **Spot instances**: There are no upfront costs for provisioning spot instances, and the costs are typically much lower than the on-demand instances. The provisioning is done through a bidding process. If you lose the bid, you will not get the EC2 instances. Usually, applications that are viable only at very low compute prices are a good use case for using spot instances.

  ▶ **Reserved instances**: These instances can be 50–60% cheaper than on-demand instances. This option is available for 1 and 3 year plans. Applications with predictable workloads that require compute instances for longer durations are a good fit for using reserved instances.

There are several AWS EC2 instance families available for different types of application workloads. These include general purpose, memory optimized, compute optimized, storage optimized, and GPU instances. Choosing the right instance type is a key decision in provisioning EC2 instances.

 Refer to `http://aws.amazon.com/ec2/instance-types/` for descriptions and typical use cases for each of these EC2 instance types.

We recommend that you start with a minimum required instance type that meets your requirements. In many cases, choosing a general-purpose EC2 instance is a good starting point. You can then load test your application on this instance for overall performance and stability. If your applications are not meeting your performance objectives on the current instance type, you can easily upgrade the size or choose a more specialized instance type, though this process does require a reboot of your instance. This approach can help you optimize your instance sizes and types.

To achieve high performance or meet compliance requirements or to just avoid noisy neighbors, the type of tenancy chosen is a critical decision. On AWS, there are two types of tenancy, dedicated and shared. In the case of dedicated tenancy, AWS provisions your instance on dedicated hardware. These instances are isolated from instances created using the shared tenancy option and instances created by other tenants. Tenancy can be configured at the instance level or at the VPC level. Once the option is selected, changing the tenancy type (instance or VPC level) is not allowed. There are cost implications of using dedicated tenancy versus shared tenancy.

In addition, if we want to set the Provisioned IOPS parameter, then we have to use the EBS-optimized instance types. Amazon EBS-optimized instances deliver dedicated throughput to Amazon EBS, with options ranging between 500 Mbps and 2,000 Mbps (depending on the instance type selected). EBS-optimized flag provides dedicated and more consistent link between EC2 and EBS. EBS optimized EC2 instances also allocate dedicated bandwidth to its attached volumes.

How to do it...

In this recipe, we will create and launch an EC2 instance.

1. After you log in to the AWS console, choose **Services**, and then select **EC2** from the list of AWS services. At this stage, the EC2 Dashboard will appear, then perform the following operations:

    1. Press the **Launch Instance** button.

2. AWS supports two types of virtualization **paravirtual** (**PV**) and **hardware virtual machine** (**HVM**). For Windows-based instances, HVM is the only option available to you. For Linux-based instances, you can use either PV or HVM. The I/O drivers, which help PV to get rid of the network and hardware emulation, are now available on HVM. Hence, HVM can give better performance than PV. Choose an AMI from the list according to your requirement.

3. Filter instance type:

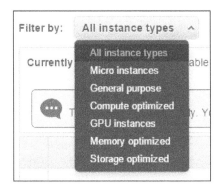

2. Choose **Columns** for more details:

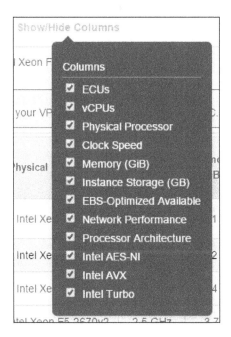

3. Choose **EBS-Optimized Available** instance type in the **Choose an Instance Type** wizard to avail this performance benefit:

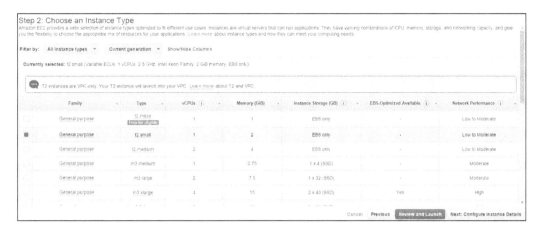

In EBS-backed instances, the root device for an instance launched using an AMI is an Amazon EBS volume created from an Amazon EBS snapshot. If we use an EBS-backed instance type, then we may or may not choose to use the instance's storage devices. We can also change the instance size, subsequently, or stop the instances to stop billing.

In case, we choose to use the instance's storage, any data stored on it will be lost after a restart of the instance. The root device for an instance launched from the AMI is an instance store volume created from a template stored in Amazon S3. We can't stop these instances—we can only terminate them. In addition, we can't change the size of instance, once created.

4. Next, we configure the VPC, subnet, and tenancy details for the instance:

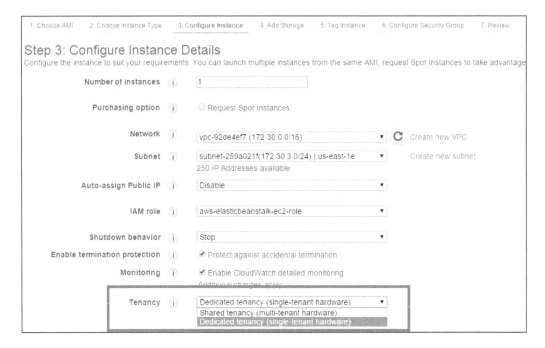

5. If you don't want to customize any further then review and launch the instance.

Preparing AWS CLI tools

AWS CLI is a set of unified command-line tools to work with multiple AWS services. Using AWS CLI tools you can manage EC2 resources (such as instances, security groups, and volumes) and your VPC resources (such as VPCs, subnets, route tables, and Internet gateways).

How to do it...

In the following two sections, we list the set of instructions required to accomplish this on Linux and Windows/Mac platforms.

Getting access key ID and secret access key

You need AWS access key ID and AWS secret access key to access AWS services. Instead of generating these credentials from the root account, it's always best practice to use IAM users. You should save these credentials in a secure location. If you lose these keys, you must delete the access key and then create a new key.

You can get the AWS credentials from AWS management portal by following these steps:

1. Log in to the AWS management portal using your AWS username and password.
2. Select account name from top menu at the right corner in the console.
3. Select security credentials.
4. Click on access keys (access key ID and secret access key).
5. Click on the **Create New Access Key** button.
6. Click on **Download Key File**, which will download the file. If you do not download the key file now, you will not be able to retrieve your secret access key again.
7. Copy this key file to a secure location.

 Don't upload your code base with AWS security credentials to public code repositories such as GitHub. Attackers are scraping GitHub for AWS credentials. If anyone gets access to these credentials, they can misuse your AWS account.

Installing AWS CLI using pip in Linux

We can use the `pip` tool to install the Python packages.

1. Before installing Python, please check whether Python is already installed on your machine or not using the following command. If Python is already installed on your machine, then skip to the `pip` installation step.

    ```
    $ python --help
    ```

2. Start by installing Python. Download the compressed TAR archive file from the Python site, and then install it using the commands listed below. The following steps target the apt-based Linux distributions:

    ```
    $ sudo apt-get install gcc
    $ wget https://www.python.org/ftp/python/2.7.8/Python-2.7.8.tgz
    $ tar -zxvf Python-2.7.8.tgz
    $ cd Python-2.7.8
    $ ./configure
    $ make
    $ sudo make install
    ```

3. Next, check the Python installation:

    ```
    $ python -help
    ```

4. Before installing `pip`, please check whether `pip` is already installed on your machine or not by using the following command. If `pip` is already installed on your machine, then skip to the `awscli` installation step:

```
$ pip -help
```

5. Move on to installing `pip`:

```
$ sudo apt-get install pip
```

6. Then install AWS CLI. If you have already installed `awscli`, you can upgrade the installation using the `-upgrade` option.

```
$ sudo pip install awscli
```

7. Next, configure AWS CLI.

   On the command prompt, type the following command, which will prompt for the `AWSAccessKey` ID, `AWSSecretKey`, default AWS region, and default output format.

```
$ sudo aws configure
```

8. Finally, check the installation by getting regions list:

```
$ sudo aws ec2 describe-regions
```

Installing AWS CLI using pip in Windows/Mac

We can use the `pip` tool to install the Python packages.

1. Before installing Python, please check whether Python is already installed on your machine or not by using the following command. If Python is already installed on your machine, then skip to the `pip` installation step.

```
$ python -help
```

2. Start by installing Python. Download the installer from the following URL and install Python by using that installer: `https://www.python.org/downloads/`.

3. Check your Python installation:

```
$ python -help
```

4. Before installing `pip`, check whether `pip` is already installed on your machine or not by using the following command. If `pip` is already installed on your machine, skip to the `awscli` installation step.

```
$ pip -help
```

5. In the next step, we install `pip`. Download and run the installation script from `https://bootstrap.pypa.io/get-pip.py`. After that, run the following command:

```
$ python get-pip.py
```

6. Install AWS CLI. If you have already installed `awscli`, you can upgrade the installation using the `-upgrade` option.

    ```
    $ pip install awscli
    ```

7. Next, we configure AWS CLI. Execute the following command from the command prompt.

    ```
    $ aws configure
    ```

    This command will then prompt you for the `AWSAccessKey` ID, `AWSSecretKey`, default AWS region, and default output format.

8. Check the installation by getting the regions list:

    ```
    $ aws ec2 describe-regions
    ```

Launching EC2 instances using EC2-Classic and EC2-VPC

Your EC2 instance receives a private IP address from the EC2-Classic range each time it's started, whereas your instance receives a static private IP address from the address range in EC2-VPC. You can only have one private IP address in EC2-Classic, but in EC2-VPC, we have multiple private IP addresses. If you attach an EIP (Elastic IP) to EC2-Classic instance, it will get dissociated when you stop the instance. But for VPC EC2 instance, it remains associated even after you stop it. We can create subnets, routing tables, and Internet gateways in VPC. For on-premise connectivity, we need VPC.

 There are different VPC options available, depending on whether you created your AWS account before or after 2013-12-04.

If you created your AWS account after 2013-12-04, then only EC2-VPC is supported. In this case, a default VPC is created in each AWS region. Therefore, unless you create your own VPC and specify it when you launch an instance, your instances are launched in your default VPC.

If you created your AWS account before 2013-03-18, then both EC2-Classic and EC2-VPC are supported in the regions you used before, and only EC2-VPC in regions that you didn't use. In this case, a default VPC is created in each region in which you haven't created any AWS resources. Therefore, unless you create your own VPC and specify it when you launch an instance in a region (that you haven't used before), the instance is launched in your default VPC for that region. However, if you launch an instance in a region that you've used before, the instance is launched in EC2-Classic.

In this recipe, we will launch EC2 instances using EC2-Classic and EC2-VPC.

Getting started...

Before we launch the EC2 instances, we need the image ID.

Run the following command to get the list of images. We can apply the filter to identify a specific image. Record the image ID for later use:

```
$ aws ec2 describe-images
--filter [Filter]
```

 You can specify one or more filters in this command.

By executing the following command, you obtain the image ID of a 64-bit version of Ubuntu 12.04 image:

```
$ aws ec2 describe-images
--filter
"Name=virtualization-type,Values=paravirtual"
"Name=root-device-type,Values=ebs" "Name=architecture,Values=x86_64"
"Name=name,Values=ubuntu/images/ebs/ubuntu-precise-12.04-amd64-
server-20130204"
```

How to do it...

We will see the EC2 instances being launched, one by one:

Launching the EC2 instance in EC2-Classic

Using the following command, we can launch instances in EC2-Classic. You can specify the number of instances to launch using the count parameter.

```
$ aws ec2 run-instances
--image-id [ImageId]
--count [InstanceCount]
--instance-type [InstanceType]
--key-name [KeyPairName]
--security-group-ids [SecurityGroupIds]
```

The parameters used in this command are described as follows:

- ▸ [ImageId]: This is the ID of the image
- ▸ [InstanceCount]: This gives number of instances to be created
- ▸ [InstanceType]: This gives the type of EC2 instance
- ▸ [KeyPairName]: This parameter provides the key/pair name for authentication
- ▸ [SecurityGroupIds]: This one provides security group IDs

The following command will create a micro instance in EC2-Classic (in the Singapore region):

```
$ aws ec2 run-instances
--image-id ami-7e2c612c
--count 1
--instance-type t1.micro
--key-name WebServerKeyPair
--security-group-ids sg-ad70b8c9
```

Launching the EC2 instance in VPC

Run the following command to launch instances in EC2-VPC. We need to specify the subnet ID while creating an instance in EC2-VPC. Before creating the instance in EC2-VPC, you have to create the VPC and subnets inside it.

```
$ aws ec2 run-instances
--image-id [ImageId]
--count [InstanceCount]
--instance-type [InstanceType]
--key-name [KeyPairName]
--security-group-ids [SecurityGroupIds]
--subnet-id [SubnetId]
```

Here, SubnetId specifies the subnet where you want to launch your instance.

Next, run the following command to create a micro instance in EC2-VPC (in the Singapore region):

```
$ aws ec2 run-instances
--image-id ami-7e2c612c
--count 1
--instance-type t1.micro
--key-name WebServerKeyPair
--security-group-ids sg-ad70b8c8
--subnet-id subnet-aed11acb
```

See also

▶ The *Configuring security groups* and *Creating an EC2 key pair* recipes

Allocating Elastic IP addresses

Elastic IP (**EIP**) address is the static public IP address. You can attach and detach the EIP from EC2 instance at any time. Instances in EC2-Classic support only one private IP address and corresponding EIP. Instances in EC2-VPC support multiple private IP addresses, and each one can have a corresponding EIP. If you stop the instance in EC2-Classic the EIP is disassociated from instance, and you have to associate it again when you start the instance. But if you stop the instance in EC2-VPC, the EIP remains associated with the EC2 instance.

In this recipe, we list the commands for allocating an Elastic IP address in a VPC and associating it with the network interface.

How to do it...

For allocating EIP addresses, perform the following steps:

1. Run the following command to allocate the EIP:

    ```
    $ aws ec2 allocate-address

    --domain [Domain]
    ```

    You have to specify whether domain is standard or VPC. Record the allocation ID for further use.

    Domain value indicates whether the EIP address is used with instances in EC2-Classic (standard) or instances in a EC2-VPC (VPC).

2. Next, run the following command to create the EIP in VPC:

    ```
    $ aws ec2 allocate-address --domain vpc
    ```

3. Then, run the following command to associate the EIP to the **Elastic Network Interface** (**ENI**):

    ```
    $ aws ec2 associate-address

    --network-interface-id [NetworkInterfaceId]

    --allocation-id [AllocationId]
    ```

    You need to provide the network interface ID of the ENI and allocation ID of the EIP you obtained in step 1. If you don't specify the private IP address, then the Elastic IP address is associated with the primary IP address.

The parameters used in this command are described here:

- ❑ [NetworkInterfaceId]: This gives the ENI ID to attach
- ❑ [AllocationId]: This provides the allocation ID of the EIP for EC2-VPC

4. Finally, run the following command to associate the EIP to ENI:

```
$ aws ec2 associate-address
--network-interface-id eni-d68df2b3
--allocation-id eipalloc-82e0ffe0
```

See also

▶ The *Creating an instance with multiple NIC cards and a static private IP address* recipe

Creating an instance with multiple NIC cards and a static private IP address

With multiple NICs, you can better manage your network traffic. Multiple NICs is one of the prerequisite for high availability. The number of NICs attached to the EC2 instance will depend on the type of EC2 instance. ENI's and multiple private IP addresses are only available for instances running in a VPC. In cases of instance failure, we can detach and then re-attach the ENI to a standby instance, where DNS changes are not required for achieving business continuity. We can attach multiple ENIs from different subnets to an instance, but they both should be in the same availability zone. This enables us to separate the public-facing traffic from the management traffic.

We can have one primary address and one or more secondary addresses for an NIC. We can detach and then attach NIC from one instance to another. We can attach one Elastic IP to each private address. When you launch an instance, a public IP address can be autoassigned to the network interface for eth0. This is possible only when you create a network interface for eth0 instead of using an existing network interface. You can detach secondary NIC (ethN) when an instance is running or stopped. However, you can't detach the primary (eth0) interface. In addition, you can attach security groups to NIC. If you set the instance termination policy to delete on termination, then the NIC will automatically be deleted, if you delete the EC2 instance.

How to do it...

Creating an instance with multiple NIC cards requires us to create a network interface, attach it to an instance, and finally associate the EIP to the ENI.

Creating a network interface

Use the following steps to create a network interface:

1. Run the following command to create the ENI. You will need to provide the subnet ID, security group IDs, and one or more private IP addresses.

   ```
   $ aws ec2 create-network-interface
   --subnet-id [SubnetId]
   --groups [SecurityGroupIds]
   --private-ip-addresses [PrivateIpAddressList]
   ```

   The parameters used in this command are described as follows:

   - `[SubnetId]`: This gives the ID of the subnet to associate with the network interface

   - `[SecurityGroupIds]`: This parameter provides IDs of one or more security groups

   - `[PrivateIpAddressList]`: This is used to show list of private IP addresses
     Syntax:

     `PrivateIpAddress=string,Primary=boolean`

2. Next, run the following command to create the ENI with private IP addresses `10.0.0.26` and `10.0.0.27`:

   ```
   $ aws ec2 create-network-interface

   --subnet-id subnet-aed11acb

   --groups sg-ad70b8c8

   --private-ip-addresses PrivateIpAddress=10.0.0.26,Primary=true PrivateIpAddress=10.0.0.27,Primary=false
   ```

In the next step, we attach the network interface to the instance.

Attaching the network interface to an instance

By running the following command, we can attach the ENI to an EC2 instance. You will need to provide the ENI ID, EC2 instance ID, and the device index.

```
$ aws ec2 attach-network-interface
--network-interface-id [NetworkInterfaceId]
--instance-id [InstanceId]
--device-index [DeviceIndex]
```

The parameters used in this command are described as follows:

- ► [NetworkInterfaceId]: This parameter provides the network interface ID to attach to an EC2 instance
- ► [InstanceId]: This one provides an EC2 instance ID
- ► [DeviceIndex]: This parameter provides the index of the device for the network interface attachment

Then, run the following command to attach the ENI to the EC2 instance:

```
$ aws ec2 attach-network-interface
--network-interface-id eni-5c88f739
--instance-id i-2e7dace3
--device-index 1
```

Associating the EIP to the ENI

By running the following command, we can associate the EIP to the ENI. You have to provide the ENI ID, EIP allocation ID, and the private address.

```
$ aws ec2 associate-address
--network-interface-id [NetworkInterfaceId]
--allocation-id [AllocationId]
--private-ip-address [PrivateIpAddress]
```

The parameters used in this command are described as follows:

- ► [NetworkInterfaceId]: This parameter provides the network interface ID to attach to an EC2 instance
- ► [AllocationId]: This gives the allocation ID of EIP, which is required for EC2-VPC
- ► [PrivateIpAddress]: If no private IP address is specified, the Elastic IP address is associated with the primary private IP address

Next, run the following command to associate the EIP to 10.0.0.26 (the private IP address of the ENI):

```
$ aws ec2 associate-address
--network-interface-id eni-5c88f739
--allocation-id eipalloc-d59f80b7
--private-ip-address 10.0.0.26
```

See also

- ► The *Configuring security groups* recipe

Selecting the right storage for your EC2 instance

Instance storage consists of disks that are physically attached to the host computer. Data on these disks is lost once the instance restarts. For persistence across restarts, we need to use EBS volumes.

EBS volumes are automatically replicated within its availability zone to protect against component failures.

AWS EBS volumes are persisted independently from your EC2 instances. These are connected through **Network Attached Storage** (**NAS**). If you lose the EC2 instance, then the data stored on EBS will still be available to a newly provisioned EC2 instance. You can attach as many EBS volumes as you want. However, an EBS volume can only be attached to one EC2 instance at a time. You can detach EBS volume from one EC2 instance, and then attach to a different EC2 instance. An I/O request of up to 256 Kilobytes is counted as a single I/O operation (IOP).

If we use standard EBS volumes as the boot device volume, then the boot process of a Windows or Linux machine is fast. We can have storage up to 16 TB and 10,000 IOPS per volume. General purpose SSD is best for boot device volumes, and small and medium sized databases. These SSD volumes can deliver a maximum throughput of 160 Mbps when attached to EBS-optimized instances.

Provisioned IOPS (SSD) volumes deliver within 10% of the IOPS performance 99.9% of the time over a given year. If we have a 200 GB volume with 1,000 IOPS, then 99.9% of the time, actual I/O on this volume will be at 900 IOPS or higher. Many database workloads need provisioned IOPS for consistent performance. We can configure storage up to 16 TB and 20,000 IOPS per volume. Provisioned IOPS volumes can deliver 320 Mbps when attached to EBS-optimized instances.

Magnetic disks are a lower cost option for EBS volumes. If data read frequency is low then this type of EBS volume is a good option.

 If you want more IOPS than what single EBS volume provides, configure the RAID array on multiple EBS volumes.

Encryption is also possible while using the EBS volumes. Encryption is done for data at rest, data in transit, and disk I/O. Using encrypted EBS volumes have a minor effect on I/O latency, but the performance remains the same. To encrypt EBS volume, you just need to select the **Encrypt this volume** checkbox when creating EBS volume from AWS console. In this recipe, we list the commands for creating an EBS volume, and then attaching it to an EC2 instance.

How to do it...

Run the following command to list the availability zones in a selected region. If the command is run in the ap-southeast-1 region, you get the list of availability zones in the Singapore region.

```
$ aws ec2 describe-availability-zones
```

Creating an EBS volume

Run the following command to create an Amazon EBS volume that can be attached to an instance in the same availability zone. Record the volume ID for further usage.

```
$ aws ec2 create-volume
--availability-zone [AvailabilityZone]
--volume-type [VolumeType]
--iops [IOPS]
--size [Size]
```

The parameters used in this command are described as follows:

  ▶ [AvailabilityZone]: This specifies the availability zone in which to create the volume. Use the describe-availability-zones command to list the availability zones.

  ▶ [VolumeType]: This gives the volume type. This can be gp2 for General Purpose (SSD) volumes, io1 for Provisioned IOPS (SSD) volumes, or standard for Magnetic volumes.

  ▶ [IOPS]: This is only valid for Provisioned IOPS (SSD) volumes. This parameter specifies the number of IOPS to provision for the volume.

  ▶ [Size]: This one gives the size of the volume, in GiBs.

Use the following command to create a 90 GiB Provisioned IOPS (SSD) volume with 1000 Provisioned IOPS in availability zone ap-southeast-1b:

```
$ aws ec2 create-volume
--availability-zone ap-southeast-1b
--volume-type io1
--iops 1000
--size 90
```

Attaching the volume

Run the following command to attach an EBS volumes to an EC2 instance. You will need to provide the EC2 instance ID, EBS volume ID, and the device name.

```
$ aws ec2 attach-volume
--volume-id [VolumeId]
--instance-id [InstanceId]
--device [Device]
```

The parameters used in this command are described as follows:

- ▶ [VolumeId] : This provides the volume ID
- ▶ [InstanceId] : This parameter gives an EC2 instance ID
- ▶ [Device] : This one is used to mention the device name to expose to the instance (for example, /dev/sdh or xvdh)

Run the following command to attach the EBS volume to an EC2 instance as /dev/sdf:

```
$ aws ec2 attach-volume
--volume-id vol-64e54f6a
--instance-id i-2e7dace3
--device /dev/sdf
```

Creating tags for consistency

Tags represent metadata for your AWS resources. Tags are used to separate your AWS resources from one another. These are key/value pairs. If we use good tags, then it's easy to filter resources by tag names. It is also helpful for analyzing your bill; we can get the billing information of all tags by filtering on tags associated with the AWS resources. For example, you can tag several resources with a specific application name, and then organize your billing information to see the total cost for that application across several AWS services. If we add a tag that has the same key as an existing tag, then the new value will override the old value. You can edit tag keys and values at any time, and you can also remove them at any time.

In this recipe, we describe the command for creating tags for our AWS resources.

How to do it...

Using the create-tags command, you can create tags for one or more AWS resources.

Creating tags for one or more AWS resources

By running the following command, you can create or update one or more tags for one or more AWS resources:

```
$ aws ec2 create-tags
--resources [Resources]
--tags [Tags]
```

The parameters used in this command are described as follows:

▶   `[Resources]`: This parameter is used to provide the IDs of one or more resources to tag

▶   `[Tags]`: This parameter provides a list of tags

Syntax:

`Key=KeyName,Value=ValueToAssign`

The following command creates the `Name` and `Group` tag with its associated value for the EC2 instance (`i-2e7dace3`):

```
$ aws ec2 create-tags

--resources i-2e7dace3

--tags

Key=Name,Value=Tomcat Key=Group,Value='FronEnd Server Group'
```

Configuring security groups

Security groups are like firewalls for your EC2 instances. If you don't specify the security group while creating instance in EC2-VPC, then AWS automatically assigns the default security group of the EC2-VPC to the instance. We can configure the inbound and outbound rules for security groups. We can also change these inbound and outbound rules while the instance is running. These changes are automatically applied.

For every VPC, we get a default security group, which we can't delete. You can't use a security group that you created for EC2-VPC when you launch an instance in EC2-Classic. You also can't use security group that you created for EC2-Classic, when you launch an instance in EC2-VPC. After you launch an instance in EC2-Classic, you can't change its security group but you can add and delete rules, which are then applied, automatically. But after you launch an instance in EC2-VPC, you can change its security groups, and add and remove rules, which are then applied, automatically.

When you specify a security group as the source or destination for a rule, the rule affects all instances associated with the security group The security groups created for EC2-Classic can only have inbound rules, but security groups created for EC2-VPC can have both inbound and outbound rules.

The limit to create security groups for each region is 500. You can create up to 100 security groups per VPC. You can also assign an unlimited number of security groups to the instance launched in EC2-Classic, whereas only 5 security groups can be assigned to an instance launched in VPC. The number of rules that can be added to each security group on EC2-Classic is 100 and for VPC it is 50.

How to do it...

In this recipe, we first list the commands for creating a security group for EC2-Classic and EC2-VPC. Then, we see how to create inbound and outbound rules. Finally, we list the command for adding the security group to an instance.

Creating a security group for EC2-Classic

By running the following command, you can create the security group in EC2-Classic. You have to provide the security group name and security group description for the security group.

```
$ aws ec2 create-security-group
--group-name [SecurityGroupName]
--description [Description]
```

The parameters used in this command are described as follows:

- ▶ [SecurityGroupName]: This provides the security group name
- ▶ [Description]: This gives the description of the security group

Next, run the following command to create a security group with the WebServerSecurityGroup name in EC2-Classic:

```
$ aws ec2 create-security-group
--group-name WebServerSecurityGroup
--description "Web Server Security Group"
```

Creating a security group for EC2-VPC

By running the following command, you can create a security group in EC2-VPC. You have to provide the security group name, security group description, and VPC ID for the security group:

```
$ aws ec2 create-security-group
--group-name [SecurityGroupName]
--description [Description]
--vpc-id [VPCId]
```

The parameters used in this command are described as follows:

- ▸ `[SecurityGroupName]`: This parameter provides the security group name
- ▸ `[Description]`: This one gives the description of the security group
- ▸ `[VPCId]`: This option provides a VPC ID

The following command will create a security group named `WebServerSecurityGroup` in VPC (vpc-1f33c27a). You can get your VPC IDs by running the `aws ec2 describe-vpcs` command.

```
$ aws ec2 create-security-group
--group-name WebServerSecurityGroup
--description "Web Server Security Group"
--vpc-id vpc-1f33c27a
```

Adding an inbound rule

Run the following command to add an inbound rule to your security group. You will need to provide the security group ID, protocol (TCP/UDP/ICMP), port, and the CIDR IP range.

```
$ aws ec2 authorize-security-group-ingress
--group-id [SecurityGroupId]
--protocol [Protocol]
--port [Port]
--cidr [CIDR]
```

The parameters used in this command are described as follows:

- ▸ `[SecurityGroupId]`: This is used to provide the security group ID
- ▸ `[Protocol]`: This one provides the IP protocol of this permission
- ▸ `[Port]`: This is used to specify the range of ports to allow
- ▸ `[CIDR]`: This one gives the CIDR IP range

Next, run the following command to create the inbound rule that allows SSH traffic from IP address 123.252.223.114 in the security group (`sg-c6b873a3`):

```
$ aws ec2 authorize-security-group-ingress
--group-id sg-c6b873a3
--protocol tcp
--port 22
--cidr 123.252.223.114/32
```

Adding an outbound rule

Run the following command to add an outbound rule to your security group. You will need to specify the security group ID, protocol (TCP/UDP/ICMP), port, and the CIDR IP range.

```
$ aws ec2 authorize-security-group-egress
--group-id [SecurityGroupId]
--protocol [Protocol]
--port [Port]
--cidr [CIDR]
```

The parameters used in this command are described as follows:

▸ [SecurityGroupId]: This parameter provides the security group ID

▸ [Protocol]: This option specifies the IP protocol of this permission

▸ [Port]: This is used to give the range of ports to allow

▸ [CIDR]: This one gives the CIDR IP range

Then, run the following command to create the outbound rule that allows MySQL traffic from your instance to IP address 123.252.223.114 in the security group (sg-c6b873a3):

```
$ aws ec2 authorize-security-group-egress
--group-id sg-c6b873a3
--protocol tcp
--port 3866
--cidr 123.252.223.114/24
```

Adding the security group to an instance

By running the following command, you can attach the security group to your EC2 instance. You have to provide the EC2 instance ID, and one or more security group IDs:

```
$ aws ec2 modify-instance-attribute
--instance-id [InstanceId]
--groups [SecurityGroupIds]
```

The parameters used in this command are described here:

▸ [InstanceId]: This option gives an EC2 instance ID

▸ [SecurityGroupIds]: This option provides the IDs of one or more security groups

Then, run the following command to add the security groups `sg-c6b873a3` and `sg-ccb873a9` to EC2 instance `i-2e7dace3`:

```
$ aws ec2 modify-instance-attribute

--instance-id i-2e7dace3

--groups sg-c6b873a3 sg-ccb873a9
```

Creating an EC2 key pair

AWS can authenticate using the public-private key mechanism. The recommended authentication mechanism is public-private key authentication instead of passwords to remotely log in to your instances with SSH. We upload the public key to AWS, and store the private key on our local machine. If anyone has your private key, then they can easily log in to your EC2 instances. It's a best practice to store these private keys in a secure place. We can create the public and private key from our machine using tools like **PuTTY Key Generator**.

You should include a passphrase with the private key to prevent unauthorized persons from logging in to your EC2 instance. When you include a passphrase, you have to enter the passphrase whenever you log in to the EC2 instance. A passphrase on a private key is an extra layer of protection. If you lost your private key for an EBS-backed instance, you can regain access to your instance by executing the following steps:

1. Stop the EBS-backed EC2 instance.
2. Detach the root volume from EC2 instance.
3. Launch the new EC2 instance for recovery.
4. Attach the EC2 root volume as data volume to the previously created instance.
5. Modify the `authorized_keys` file.
6. Detach the root volume from recovery instance.
7. Attach the root volume back to the EC2 instance.
8. Start the instance.

How to do it...

Here, we list the commands to create a key pair and then launching the EC2 instance (using the key pair).

Creating a key pair

Use the following steps to create a key pair:

1. Run the following command to create the key pair.

    You have to provide the key pair name. You can explicitly specify the text output for this command using the -output argument for easy cut and paste.

    ```
    $ aws ec2 create-key-pair
    --key-name [KeyPairName]
    ```

     The [KeyPairName] parameter in this command is used to specify a name for the key pair.

2. After executing the create-key-pair command, copy the entire output key into file including the following lines:

    ```
    ----BEGIN RSA PRIVATE KEY----
    -----END RSA PRIVATE KEY-----
    ```

3. Save the file with ASCII encoding.

4. Run the following command to create the key pair with name WebServerKeyPair.

    ```
    $ aws ec2 create-key-pair
    --key-name WebServerKeyPair
    ```

Grouping EC2 instances using placement groups

EC2 instances can be grouped using placement groups. For example, instances requiring low latency and high bandwidth communication can be placed in the same placement group. When instances are placed in this placement group, they have access to low latency, non-blocking 10 Gbps networking when communicating with other instances in the placement group (within a single availability zone). AWS recommends launching all the instances within the cluster placement group at the same time.

How to do it...

In order to group EC2 instances using placement groups, first we create a placement group, and then add our EC2 instances in it.

Creating a placement group

Run the following command to create placement groups. You have to provide the placement group name and the placement strategy.

```
$ aws ec2 create-placement-group
--group-name [GroupName]
--strategy [Strategy]
```

Here, the `GroupName` parameter specifies a name for the placement group and the `Strategy` parameter specifies the placement strategy.

Next, run the following command to create a placement group with the name `WebServerGroup`:

```
$ aws ec2 create-placement-group
--group-name WebServerGroup
--strategy cluster
```

Placing instances in the placement group

Run the following command to launch instances in a placement group. You will need to specify the placement group name along with the EC2 instance properties.

```
$ aws ec2 run-instances
--image-id [ImageId]
--count [Count]
--instance-type [InstanceType]
--key-name [KeyPairName]
--security-group-ids [SecurityGroupIds]
--subnet-id [SubnetId]
--placement [Placement]
```

The parameters used in this command are described as follows:

- ► `[ImageId]`: This gives the ID of the image from which you want to create the EC2 instance
- ► `[Count]`: This one provides the number of instances to create
- ► `[InstanceType]`: This option gives the type of EC2 instance
- ► `[KeyPairName]`: This parameter provides the key pair name for the authentication
- ► `[SecurityGroupIds]`: This parameter gives one or more security group IDs
- ► `[SubnetId]`: This option provides the ID of the subnet where you want to launch your instance

▶ [Placement]: This gives the placement for the instance.

Syntax:

```
--placement AvailabilityZone=value,GroupName=value,Tenancy=value
```

Next, execute the following command to launch a c3.large EC2 instance in the WebServerGroup placement group:

```
$ aws ec2 run-instances
--image-id ami-7e2c612c
--count 1
--instance-type c3.large
--key-name WebServerKeyPair
--security-group-ids sg-ad70b8c8
--subnet-id subnet-aed11acb
--placement GroupName= WebServerGroup
```

Configuring Elastic Load Balancing

The **Elastic Load Balancer** (**ELB**) works within a single AWS region. You can scale both horizontally (adding more EC2 instances) and vertically (increasing EC2 instance size) within AWS, but it's best practice to scale horizontally. It can, however, load balance across several instances in multiple availability zones. If you don't want to load balance instances across multiple availability zones, then you can also disable it. If we want to load balance the instances across multiple regions, then we have to use Route 53 (instead of an ELB). ELB continuously checks the health of the instances, and only routes traffic to healthy instances. The health check frequency and the URL parameters are configurable.

If a healthy instance comes online, then the ELB recognizes the instance and routes traffic to it. ELB can be used to implement high-availability application architectures. If we use Route 53 with ELB, we can enable failover to a different region. ELB can also be configured with autoscaling, thereby enabling load balancing across new instances created by auto-scaling groups.

ELB can work with instances in EC2-Classic and VPC. There are two types of load balancers we can create internal or internet facing. We can't create internal load balancer without VPC. We can create both internal and internet facing load balancers within VPC. You can also enable sticky sessions on ELB using either application generated cookies or ELB generated cookies. In addition, you can assign security groups to ELBs. If you don't assign any security group while creating the ELB in VPC, it uses the default security group of the VPC. SSL termination is also supported in ELB, using this obviates the need to install SSL certificate on each and every EC2 instance.

How to do it...

Here, we list the commands for creating an ELB, configuring the same for performing health checks, and finally associating specific EC2 instances with it.

Creating an Internet-facing ELB with listeners

Run the following command to create an Internet-facing ELB. You will have to provide the listeners, subnet IDs, and security group IDs.

```
$ aws elb create-load-balancer
--load-balancer-name [LoanBalancerName]
--listeners [Listeners]
--subnets [SubnetIds]
--security-groups [SecurityGroups]
```

The parameters used in this command are described as follows:

- ▶ `[LoanBalancerName]`: This option provides the name of the load balancer.
- ▶ `[Listeners]`: This parameter gives a list of the following tuples: `Protocol`, `LoadBalancerPort`, `InstanceProtocol`, `InstancePort`, and `SSLCertificateId`.
- ▶ `[SubnetIds]`: This option gives a list of subnet IDs in your VPC to attach to your load balancer. You can get a list of subnet IDs by running the `aws ec2 describe-subnets` command.
- ▶ `[SecurityGroups]`: This option provides the security groups to assign to your load balancer within your VPC. You can get security group ID by running the `aws ec2 describe-security-groups` command. You should provide the security group name in the preceding command.

Run the following command to create an ELB that receives traffic on port 80, and the load balances across instances listening on port 8080:

```
$ aws elb create-load-balancer
--load-balancer-name WebLoadBalancer
--listeners
Protocol=HTTP,LoadBalancerPort=80,InstanceProtocol=HTTP,InstancePort=8080
--subnets subnet-aed11acb
--security-groups sg-c6b873a3
```

Configuring health checks on ELB

Run the following command to add health check configuration to an ELB. You have to provide the load balancer name and health check configuration:

```
$ aws elb configure-health-check
--load-balancer-name [LoanBalancerName]
--health-check [HealthCheckup]
```

The parameters used in this command are described as follows:

- ▸ [LoanBalancerName]: This option provides the name of the load balancer
- ▸ [HealthCheckup]: This parameter provides the health check configuration

  Syntax:

  ```
  Target=HTTP:8080/index.html,Interval=30,UnhealthyThreshold=
  2,HealthyThreshold=2,Timeout=3
  ```

The following command will add the health check configuration to an ELB. The ELB checks the instance health at <URL>:8080/index.html. ELB health check interval is set to 30 seconds. UnhealthyThreshold specifies the number of consecutive unsuccessful URL probes before the ELB changes the instance health status to unhealthy. HealthyThreshold specifies the number of consecutive successful URL probes before ELB changes the instance health status to healthy.

```
$ aws elb configure-health-check
--load-balancer-name WebLoadBalancer
--health-check Target=HTTP:8080/index.html,Interval=30,UnhealthyThreshold
=2,HealthyThreshold=2,Timeout=3
```

Adding instances to the ELB

By running the following command, you can add instances to the ELB. You have to provide the ELB name and the list of instance IDs.

```
$ aws elb register-instances-with-load-balancer
--load-balancer-name [LoanBalancerName]
--instances [Instances]
```

The parameters used in this command are described as follows:

- ▸ [LoanBalancerName]: This option gives the name of the load balancer
- ▸ [Instances]: This option gives a list of instances for the load balancer

The following command will add ELB to EC2 instances with IDs `i-d3ff2c1e` and `i-2e7dace3`.

```
$ aws elb register-instances-with-load-balancer
--load-balancer-name WebLoadBalancer
--instances i-d3ff2c1e i-2e7dace3
```

Architecting for high availability

Application and network errors can render the system unavailable to the user. Multi-availability zone deployments are used for building high-availability applications at the AWS region level. For implementing fault tolerance for region level failures, we have to deploy our application in availability zones spanning across different regions. If we use multiple regions, we have to use Route 53 for failover. If the primary region goes down, Route 53 fails over to the secondary region.

Increasing load on system can also cause system availability issues, but the autoscaling feature can help us solve the problem by autoscaling the number of servers during a spike in load. The number of servers is automatically reduced when the load comes back to normal levels. Detailed explanation on autoscaling is in *Chapter 3, Managing AWS Resources Using AWS CloudFormation*.

Building loosely coupled applications can also help avoid single points of failure. We can use **Simple Queue Service** (**SQS**) to build loosely coupled applications. Using the SQS queue size as a parameter, we can auto-scale our EC2 instances. For RDS high availability, we can configure a multi availability zone-deployment option. This will deploy the primary and secondary database instances in two different availability zones.

How to do it...

Here, we list the commands required for configuring high availability across two different regions using Route 53:

1. Create an instance in the first region. Before launching the EC2 instance, create the required VPC, subnets, key pairs, and security groups in this region.

    ```
    $ aws ec2 run-instances
    --image-id [ImageId]
    --count [InstanceCount]
    --instance-type [InstanceType]
    --key-name [KeyPairName]
    --security-group-ids [SecurityGroupIds]
    --subnet-id [SubnetId]
    ```

The parameters used in this command are described as follows:

- ❏ [ImageId]: This option gives the ID of the image
- ❏ [InstanceCount]: This parameter provides the number of instances to create
- ❏ [InstanceType]: This parameter provides the type of EC2 instance
- ❏ [KeyPairName]: This gives a key/pair name for authentication
- ❏ [SecurityGroupIds]: This option provides the security group ID
- ❏ [SubnetId]: This parameter provides the ID of subnet where you want to launch your instance

2. Create an instance in the second region. Before launching the EC2 instance, create the required VPC, subnets, key pairs, and security groups in this region:

```
$ aws ec2 run-instances
--image-id [ImageId]
--count [InstanceCount]
--instance-type [InstanceType]
--key-name [KeyPairName]
--security-group-ids [SecurityGroupIds]
--subnet-id [SubnetId]
```

The parameters used in this command are described as follows:

- ❏ [ImageId]: This parameter provides the ID of the image
- ❏ [InstanceCount]: This option gives the number of instances to create
- ❏ [InstanceType]: This one gives the type of EC2 instance
- ❏ [KeyPairName]: This parameter provides a key/pair name for authentication
- ❏ [SecurityGroupIds]: This option gives a security group ID
- ❏ [SubnetId]: This parameter provides the ID of the subnet where you want to launch your instance

3. Create an AWS hosted zone in Route 53 service.

The following command will return the name server records. Record the name server records and the hosted zone ID for the further usage.

```
$ aws route53 create-hosted-zone
--name [Name]
--caller-reference [CallReference]
```

The parameters used in this command are described as follows:

- ❏ [Name]: This parameter gives the name of the domain
- ❏ [CallReference]: This parameter gives a unique string that identifies the request and that allows failed `create-hosted-zone` requests to be retried without the risk of executing the operation twice

Change the name servers records with your domain registrar.

> Use the following link to understand how to change name servers with GoDaddy:
>
> `https://support.godaddy.com/help/article/664/`
> `setting-nameservers-for-your-domain-names`

4. Create health checks for previously created instances in the first region by performing the following steps:

    1. First create a `virginiahc.json` file with the following JSON. The IP address used is the public IP address of EC2 instance.

       ```
       {
       "IPAddress":"54.173.200.169",
       "Port":8080,
       "Type":"HTTP",
       "ResourcePath":"/index.html",
       "RequestInterval":30,
       "FailureThreshold":3
       }
       ```

    2. Execute the following command for the first region:

       ```
       $ aws route53 create-health-check
       --caller-reference [CallReference]
       --health-check-config [HealthCheckConfig]
       ```

       The parameters used in this command are described as follows:

       - ❏ [CallReference]: This is a unique string that identifies the request and that allows failed `create-health-check` requests to be retried without the risk of executing the operation twice
       - ❏ [HealthCheckConfig]: This option gives the health check configuration

         Syntax:

         `file://virginiahc.json`

3. Create health check by running the following command. Record the health check ID for further usage.

```
$ aws route53 create-health-check
--caller-reference 2014-11-29-17:03
--health-check-config file://virginiahc.json
```

5. Create health checks for previously created instances in second region by performing the following steps:

1. Create a second `singaporehc.json` file with the following JSON. The IP address used is the public IP address of EC2 instance.

```
{
"IPAddress":"54.169.85.163",
"Port":8080,
"Type":"HTTP",
"ResourcePath":"/index.html",
"RequestInterval":30,
"FailureThreshold":3
}
```

2. Execute the following command for the second region:

```
$ aws route53 create-health-check
--caller-reference [CallReference]
--health-check-config [HealthCheckConfig]
```

The parameters used in this command are described as follows:

❏ `[CallReference]`: A unique string that identifies the request and that allows failed `create-health-check` requests to be retried without the risk of executing the operation twice

❏ `[HealthCheckConfig]`: This option provides the health check configuration

Syntax:

```
file:// singaporehc.json
```

3. Create health check by running the following command. Record the health check ID for further usage.

```
$ aws route53 create-health-check
--caller-reference 2014-11-29-17:04
--health-check-config file://singaporehc.json
```

6. Add a primary and secondary record set to the Route 53-hosted zone by performing the following steps:

    1. Create a `recordset.json` file with the following JSON. In primary record set, replace health check ID and IP address with first region health check ID and EC2 public IP address accordingly. In secondary record set, replace health check ID and IP address with second region health check ID and EC2 public IP address accordingly.

```json
{
    "Comment":"Creating Record Set",
    "Changes":[
        {
            "Action":"CREATE",
            "ResourceRecordSet":{
                "Name":"DNS Domain Name",
                "Type":"A",
                "SetIdentifier":"PrimaryRecordSet",
                "Failover":"PRIMARY",
                "TTL":300,
                "ResourceRecords":[
                    {
                        "Value":"54.173.200.169"
                    }
                ],
                "HealthCheckId":"<your first region's
                health check id>"
            }
        },
        {
            "Action":"CREATE",
            "ResourceRecordSet":{
                "Name":" DNS Domain Name",
                "Type":"A",
                "SetIdentifier":"SecondaryRecordSet",
                "Failover":"SECONDARY",
                "TTL":300,
                "ResourceRecords":[
                    {
                        "Value":"54.169.85.163"
                    }
                ],
                "HealthCheckId":"<your second region's
                health check id>"
            }
        }
    ]
}
```

2. Execute the following command to add record set:

```
$ aws route53 change-resource-record-sets
--hosted-zone-id [HostedZoneId]
--change-batch [ChangeBatch]
```

The parameters used in this command are described as follows:

❏ [HostedZoneId]: This option provides the Route 53-hosted zone ID

❏ [ChangeBatch]: A complex type that contains an optional comment and the changes element

Syntax:

```
file://recordset.json
```

3. Add the record set to the hosted zone by running the following command:

```
$ aws route53 change-resource-record-sets
--hosted-zone-id Z3DYG8V5Z07JP8
--change-batch file://recordset.json
```

7. Test the failover configuration by stopping the server in the primary region. You can stop your first region EC2 instance by running the `aws ec2 stop-instances` command.

Creating instances for AWS Marketplace

The AWS Marketplace helps customers find software from a set of third-party vendors. There is no need to set up a new billing account for another company; those bills can be paid via the AWS monthly bills. We can read reviews from other customers to help us make the most appropriate selection. We can also share or sell our AMIs with the public so that the wider community can use them.

In this recipe, we list the commands for creating AMIs for offering them to other users on AWS Marketplace.

How to do it...

Here we list the commands for creating AMIs for offering them to other users on AWS Marketplace.

Creating an AMI from EC2 instance

By running the following command, you can create the image from EC2 instance. You have to provide the instance ID, image name, and image description.

```
$ aws ec2 create-image
```

```
--instance-id [InstanceId]
--name [Name]
--description [Description]
```

The parameters used in this command are described as follows:

- ▶ [InstanceId]: This option provides the EC2 instance ID
- ▶ [Name]: This option gives the name of the image
- ▶ [Description]: This one provides the image description

The following command creates an image of the EC2 instance with ID i-2e7dace3:

```
$ aws ec2 create-image
--instance-id i-2e7dace3
--name "WebServerImage"
--description "Image of web server"
```

Making the AMI public

By running the following command, you can make your image public. You have to provide the image ID and launch permissions.

```
$ aws ec2 modify-image-attribute
--image-id [ImageId]
--launch-permission [LaunchPermission]
```

The parameters used in this command are described as follows:

- ▶ [ImageId]: This option provides the image ID
- ▶ [LaunchPermission]: This option is used to launch permissions
  Syntax:
  "{\"Add\": [{\"Group\":\"all\"}]}"

By running following command, you can make your image public.

```
$ aws ec2 modify-image-attribute
--image-id ami-97e6cbc5
--launch-permission "{\"Add\": [{\"Group\":\"all\"}]}"
```

2

Configuring and Securing a Virtual Private Cloud

In this chapter, we will cover recipes for:

- ▶ Creating and configuring VPC
- ▶ Configuring VPC DHCP options
- ▶ Configuring networking connections between two VPCs (VPC peering)
- ▶ Connecting your on-premise network to VPC using VPN

Introduction

In this chapter, we will focus on recipes to create and configure AWS VPC (Virtual Private Cloud) against typical network infrastructure requirements. VPCs help you isolate AWS EC2 resources, and this feature is available in all AWS regions. A VPC can span multiple availability zones in a region. AWS VPC also helps you run hybrid applications on AWS by extending your existing datacenter into the public cloud. Disaster recovery is another common use case for using AWS VPC. You can create subnets, routing tables, and internet gateways in VPC. By creating public and private subnets, you can put your web and frontend services in the public subnet, while your application databases and backed services are located in a private subnet. Using VPN, you can extend your on-premise data center. Another option to extend your on-premise datacenter is AWS Direct Connect, which is a private network connection between AWS and your on-premise datacenter. In VPC, EC2 resources get static private IP addresses that persist across reboots, which works in the same way as the DHCP reservation.

You can also assign multiple IP addresses and Elastic Network Interfaces. You can have a private ELB accessible only within your VPC. You can use CloudFormation to automate the VPC creation process. Defining appropriate tags can help you manage your VPC resources more efficiently.

We will start with a recipe to create and configure a VPC and then follow it up with recipes to configure DHCP, and connect two VPCs as well as your on-premise network to your AWS VPC, in the following sections.

Creating and configuring VPC

In this section, we present the recipe to create and configure a VPC. You can assign a single **Classless Inter-Domain Routing** (**CIDR**) block to the VPC. The allowed block size is between a /28 (16 IP addresses) net mask and /16 (65536 IP addresses) net mask. Public and private subnets are specified to build multitier applications. To access the Internet from a private subnet, we have to use **Network Address Translation** (**NAT**) instance in the public subnet. Each subnet must be associated with a routing table. Each route in the routing table contains the destination CIDR network range and a target Internet gateway/virtual private gateway.

To access the Internet the EC2 instance must either have an **Elastic IP** (**EIP**) address or a public IP address. You can also use a NAT instance, which will have a public IP address and perform the natting for your instances. Your subnet's route table must contain the route that directs the Internet bound traffic to the Internet gateway. You have to ensure that network **Access Control List** (**ACL**) and security groups allow the Internet traffic to and from your instance. To access the on-premise servers or other AWS instances outside your VPC, you can add public IP addresses of those servers as destination and the Internet gateway as the target in your subnet routing table.

Network ACL operates at a subnet level. Network ACL controls the subnet's inbound and outbound traffic. We can configure inbound and outbound rules for network ACL, which are then evaluated in order. As network ACLs are stateless, you have to explicitly add rules for return traffic. We can use network ACL as an additional layer of security along with the security groups. Each subnet must be associated with the network ACL. If you don't specify the network ACL, then it will be automatically associated with the default network ACL.

How to do it...

Here, we present specific commands to use for creating and configuring a VPC, including creating a VPC with a CIDR block and dedicated tenancy, adding tags for your VPC, and viewing the details of the newly created VPC. We then create private and public subnets, security group for the NAT instance, a NAT instance, an Internet gateway, and route tables for the private and public subnets. Finally, we test our VPC setup.

1. Create a VPC with CIDR block and dedicated tenancy.

   The following command creates a VPC setup with a CIDR network range of 10.0.0.0/16 in dedicated tenancy. Record the VPC ID for further use.

   ```
   $ aws ec2 create-vpc

   --cidr-block 10.0.0.0/16

   --instance-tenancy dedicated
   ```

   Add tags to the VPC.

   ```
   $ aws ec2 create-tags

   --resources vpc-0214e967

   --tags Key=Name,Value=TestVPC
   ```

2. Describe the VPC.

   ```
   $ aws ec2 describe-vpcs

   --vpc-ids vpc-0214e9670214e9670214e967
   ```

3. Create public and private subnets in VPC by performing the following steps:

   1. Execute the following command to create a subnet with the name `PublicSubnet`. This subnet provides 256 private IP addresses. Please select availability zone as per your requirement.

      ```
      $ aws ec2 create-subnet

      --vpc-id vpc-0214e967

      --cidr-block 10.0.0.0/24

      --availability-zone ap-southeast-1a
      ```

   2. Associate the name with this subnet.

      ```
      $ aws ec2 create-tags

      --resources subnet-0240b575

      --tags Key=Name,Value=PublicSubnet
      ```

   3. Create a subnet with the name `PrivateSubnet`. Provide the availability zone as per your requirements.

      ```
      $ aws ec2 create-subnet

      --vpc-id vpc-0214e967

      --cidr-block 10.0.1.0/24

      --availability-zone ap-southeast-1a
      ```

4. Associate the name with this subnet.

```
$ aws ec2 create-tags
--resources subnet-49ca1b2c
--tags Key=Name,Value=PrivateSubnet
```

4. Create a security group for the NAT instance and inbound and outbound rules for the ports.

```
$ aws ec2 create-security-group
--group-name NATSecurityGroup
--description "NAT Server Security Group"
--vpc-id vpc-0214e967
```

1. Add inbound rules for port 80 and 443 from `PrivateSubnet` and 22 from the public IP range of your network. `WhatsMyIp` will return the public IP address of your workstation. Allow access only from the specified IP address, by specifying /32 with the IP address.

```
$ aws ec2 authorize-security-group-ingress
--group-id sg-5173a334
--protocol tcp
--port 22
--cidr 123.252.223.114/32


$ aws ec2 authorize-security-group-ingress
--group-id sg-5173a334
--protocol tcp
--port 80
--cidr 10.0.1.0/24


$ aws ec2 authorize-security-group-ingress
--group-id sg-5173a334
--protocol tcp
--port 443
--cidr 10.0.1.0/24
```

2. Add the outbound rules for 80 and 443. This allows outbound HTTP and HTTPS access to the Internet over the Internet gateway.

```
$ aws ec2 authorize-security-group-egress
--group-id sg-5173a334
```

```
--protocol tcp
--port 80
--cidr 0.0.0.0/0

$ aws ec2 authorize-security-group-egress
--group-id sg-5173a334
--protocol tcp
--port 443
--cidr 0.0.0.0/0
```

5. Create and launch a NAT instance in the public subnet by performing the
    following steps:

    1. Get the list of Amazon NAT instance images. Use the most recent AMI from
        the list of AMI's.

        ```
        $ aws ec2 describe-images
        --filter Name="owner-alias",Values="amazon"
        --filter Name="name",Values="amzn-ami-vpc-nat*"
        ```

    2. Create a key/pair for the NAT instance.

        ```
        $ aws ec2 create-key-pair
        --key-name NATServerKeyPair
        ```

    3. Launch the NAT instance in the public subnet.

        ```
        $ aws ec2 run-instances
        --image-id ami-70a38222
        --count 1
        --instance-type t1.micro
        --key-name NATServerKeyPair
        --security-group-ids sg-5173a334
        --subnet-id subnet-0240b575
        ```

    4. Associate a name with the NAT instance.

        ```
        $ aws ec2 create-tags
        --resources i-1634e7da
        --tags Key=Name,Value=NATInstance
        ```

    5. Disable source/destination check.

        ```
        $ aws ec2 modify-instance-attribute
        --instance-id i-1634e7da
        --source-dest-check "{\"Value\": false}"
        ```

6. Create the EIP in VPC.

```
$ aws ec2 allocate-address
--domain vpc
```

7. Associate EIP with the NAT instance.

```
$ aws ec2 associate-address
--instance-id i-1634e7da
--allocation-id eipalloc-37302855
```

6. Create an Internet gateway by performing the following steps:

1. Execute the following command to create an Internet gateway.

```
$ aws ec2 create-internet-gateway
```

2. Attach the Internet gateway to the VPC.

```
$ aws ec2 attach-internet-gateway
--internet-gateway-id igw-95c22df0
--vpc-id vpc-0214e967
```

7. Create a route table for the private subnet

1. Execute the following command to create a route table for `PrivateSubnet`.

```
$ aws ec2 create-route-table
--vpc-id vpc-0214e967
```

2. Associate a name with the route table.

```
$ aws ec2 create-tags
--resources rtb-7c18d919
--tags Key=Name,Value=PrivateRouteTable
```

3. Add a route in the route table, which routes all traffic to the NAT instance.

```
$ aws ec2 create-route
--route-table-id rtb-7c18d919
--destination-cidr-block 0.0.0.0/0
--instance-id i-1634e7da
```

4. Associate the route table.

```
$ aws ec2 associate-route-table
--route-table-id rtb-7c18d919
--subnet-id subnet-49ca1b2c
```

8. Create a route table for the public subnet.

   1. Execute the following command to create a route table for `PublicSubnet`.

      ```
      $ aws ec2 create-route-table
      --vpc-id vpc-0214e967
      ```

   2. Associate a name with the route table.

      ```
      $ aws ec2 create-tags
      --resources rtb-7f1bda1a
      --tags Key=Name,Value=PublicRouteTable
      ```

   3. Add a route in the route table that routes all traffic to the Internet gateway.

      ```
      $ aws ec2 create-route
      --route-table-id rtb-7f1bda1a
      --destination-cidr-block 0.0.0.0/0
      --gateway-id igw-95c22df0
      ```

   4. Associate the route table with the subnet.

      ```
      $ aws ec2 associate-route-table
      --route-table-id rtb-7f1bda1a
      --subnet-id subnet-0240b575
      ```

9. Test the setup.

   1. Launch an instance in `PublicSubnet` with a security group that allows SSH traffic from the public IP range of your network.

      ```
      $ aws ec2 create-security-group
      --group-name PublicServerSecurityGroup
      --description "Public Server Security Group"
      --vpc-id vpc-0214e967
      ```

   2. Add an inbound rule for port 22 that allows traffic from the public IP range of your network.

      ```
      $ aws ec2 authorize-security-group-ingress
      --group-id sg-0a76a66f
      --protocol tcp
      --port 22
      --cidr 123.252.223.114/32
      ```

   3. Create a key pair

      ```
      $ aws ec2 create-key-pair
      --key-name PublicServerKeyPair
      ```

4. Launch the instance in `PublicSubnet`.

    ```
    $ aws ec2 run-instances
    --image-id ami-7e2c612c
    --count 1
    --instance-type t1.micro
    --key-name PublicServerKeyPair
    --security-group-ids sg-0a76a66f
    --subnet-id subnet-0240b575
    ```

5. Launch an instance in the private subnet with a security group that allows SSH traffic from the public subnet only.

    ```
    $ aws ec2 create-security-group
    --group-name PrivateServerSecurityGroup
    --description "Private Server SecurityGroup"
    --vpc-id vpc-0214e967
    ```

6. Add an inbound rule for port 22 that allows traffic from `PublicSubnet` only.

    ```
    $ aws ec2 authorize-security-group-ingress
    --group-id sg-d476a6b1
    --protocol tcp
    --port 22
    --cidr 10.0.0.0/24
    ```

7. Create a key pair.

    ```
    $ aws ec2 create-key-pair
    --key-name PrivateServerKeyPair
    ```

8. Launch the instance in `PrivateSubnet`.

    ```
    $ aws ec2 run-instances
    --image-id ami-7e2c612c
    --count 1
    --instance-type t1.micro
    --key-name PrivateServerKeyPair
    --security-group-ids sg-d476a6b1
    --subnet-id subnet-49ca1b2c
    ```

How it works...

We first created a VPC with dedicated tenancy by specifying the network range for the VPC, in the CIDR notation. Each instance launched in a VPC has a tenancy attribute and each VPC has a related instance tenancy attribute. As we created our VPC with the dedicated attribute, all instances launched in this VPC will be dedicated instances irrespective of the value of the instance's tenancy attribute. Note that some instance types cannot be launched in a VPC with the tenancy attribute set to dedicated. The tenancy information for the VPC is displayed on the VPC console.

Next, we created a tag to help us identify our VPC resource by associating our own metadata with it. Tags are specified as key/value pairs. For our VPC, we specify the key as name and assign `TestVPC` as the value. You can specify other tags to categorize your VPC or other AWS resources, for example, you can specify the owner or primary contact for the resource and the environment (dev, test, staging, production, and so on), to better manage the resources in your account.

Then, we retrieved the description of our VPC to verify the VPC ID, tenancy (default or dedicated), tags specified (both key and value), current state of the VPC (pending or available), the CIDR block, and an indicator whether the VPC is the default VPC (true or false). In addition, executing the `describe-vpcs` command also returns the ID of the DHCP options set associated with your VPC. To assign your own domain name to your instances, you must specify the appropriate DHCP options to use with the VPC. The DHCP option sets are associated with your AWS account.

We created public and private subnets by dividing the VPC CIDR block, and specifying the appropriate availability zone. In our example, we ensure that the CIDR blocks for our subnets do not overlap. If you are defining a single subnet in your VPC, then the CIDR block of your subnet is the same as that for the VPC. Though VPCs can span multiple availability zones, each subnet must reside entirely within one availability zone. In our example, we placed our subnets in the same availability zone, however, you can choose to place your subnets in separate availability zones to protect against availability zone failures. In this step, we also create tags to name our subnets `PublicSubnet` and `PrivateSubnet`.

Next, we create a security group for our NAT instance with inbound and outbound rules for specific ports. The inbound rules allow inbound HTTP traffic on port 80 from servers in the private subnet, HTTPS traffic on port 443 from servers in the private subnet, and inbound SSH access to the NAT instance from a specific IP your network. The outbound rules allow outbound HTTP and HTTPS access to the Internet on ports 80 and 443, respectively.

In the next step, we create and launch a NAT instance. We use the NAT instance in the public subnet of our VPC to enable instances in the private subnet to initiate outbound traffic to the Internet while preventing inbound traffic (from the Internet). We start by executing the `describe-images` command that describes one or more images, that is, AMIs available for you to launch. We filter the results of this command to retrieve Amazon AMIs that are configured to run as NAT instances. The AMI names contain the `amzn-ami-vpc-nat` string with a version number, so we filter the results using this string and choose the most recent AMI for our use. At this stage, we create a key pair and launch our NAT instance in the public subnet with the previously created security group.

We have chosen a micro instance in our example, however, you should choose the NAT instance type based on your intended load. If your application connects to the Internet occasionally and does not require high-network bandwidth, then a micro instance might suffice. However, if your application communicates with the Internet constantly and requires higher bandwidth, then a medium or a large instance may be required.

We can use the `describe-instances` command to check the state of our instance. It should be in a running state before we proceed with the next steps. As EC2 instances perform source/destination checks by default, that is, an instance must be the source or destination of any traffic it sends or receives. However, a NAT server must be able to send and receive traffic from sources or destinations other than itself. Therefore, we use the `modify-instance-attribute` command to disable the source/destination checks for our NAT instance.

In the next step, we allocate an EIP address for use with instances in our VPC. The EIP is associated with our AWS account, and helps in dynamically remapping the address to another instance in our account in case of instance failures. We associate this EIP address with our NAT instance.

The next set of commands creates an Internet gateway and attaches the same to our VPC. This step enables Internet access for instances in our subnets. The NAT instance is connected to the Internet using the Internet gateway. For example, an instance in the private subnet can connect to the Internet via the NAT instance, which routes traffic from/to the instance using the Internet gateway.

In the next two steps we create custom route tables for our private and public subnets. These route tables explicitly control the routing for each subnet's outbound traffic. After creating a route table we define routes and associate them with our subnets. Each route specifies a destination CIDR and a target (for example, we route all traffic to the NAT instance in the private subnet and to the Internet gateway in the public subnet). As a practice, we should use the most specific route when determining how to route our traffic. For example, if we have two routes to the same destination then the route that covers a smaller number of IP addresses is used.

Finally, we test our VPC by creating instances in our public and private subnets.

Configuring VPC DHCP options

DHCP options sets are associated with your AWS account so that they can be used across all your VPCs. You can assign your own domain name to your instances by specifying a set of DHCP options for your VPC. However, only one DHCP option set can be associated with a VPC. Also, you can't modify the DHCP option set after it is created. In case you want to use a different set of DHCP options then you will need to create a new DHCP option set and associate it with your VPC. There is no need to restart or relaunch the instances in the VPC after associating the new DHCP option set as they can automatically pick up the changes.

How to do it...

In this section, we will create a DHCP option set and then associate it with your VPC.

1. Create a DHCP option set with a specific domain name and domain name servers. In our example, we execute commands to create a DHCP options set and associate it with our VPC. We specify domain name `testdomain.com` and DNS servers (`10.2.5.1` and `10.2.5.2`) as our DHCP options.

    ```
    $ aws ec2 create-dhcp-options

    --dhcp-configuration Key=domain-name,Values=testdomain.com
    Key=domain-name-servers,Values=10.2.5.1,10.2.5.2
    ```

2. Associate the DHCP option set to your VPC (`vpc-bb936ede`).

    ```
    $ aws ec2 associate-dhcp-options

    --dhcp-options-id dopt-dc7d65be

    --vpc-id vpc-bb936ede
    ```

How it works...

DHCP provides a standard for passing configuration information to hosts in a network. The DHCP message contains an options field in which parameters such as the domain name and the domain name servers can be specified. By default, instances in AWS are assigned an unresolvable host name, hence we need to assign our own domain name and use our own DNS servers. The DHCP options sets are associated with the AWS account and can be used across our VPCs.

First, we create a DHCP option set. In this step, we specify the DHCP configuration parameters as key/value pairs where commas separate the values and multiple pairs are separated by spaces. In our example, we specify two domain name servers and a domain name. We can use up to four DNS servers. Next, we associate the DHCP option set with our VPC to ensure that all the existing and new instances launched in our VPC will use this DHCP options set.

Note that if you want to use a different set of DHCP options, then you will need to create a new set and again associate them with your VPC as modifications to a set of DHCP options is not allowed. In addition, you can let the instances pick up the changes automatically or explicitly renew the DHCP lease. However, in all cases only one set of DHCP options can be associated with a VPC at any given time. As a practice, delete the DHCP options set when none of your VPCs are using it and you don't need it any longer.

Configuring networking connections between two VPCs (VPC peering)

In this recipe, we will configure VPC peering. VPC peering helps you connect instances in two different VPCs using their private IP addresses. VPC peering is limited to within a region. However, you can create a VPC peering connection between VPCs that belong to different AWS accounts. The two VPCs that participate in VPC peering must not have matching or overlapping CIDR addresses. To create a VPC connection, the owner of the local VPC has to send the request to the owner of the peer VPC located in the same account or a different account. Once the owner of peer VPC accepts the request, the VPC peering connection is activated. You will need to update the routes in your route table to send traffic to the peer VPC and vice versa. You will also need to update your instance security groups to allow traffic from-to the peer VPC.

How to do it...

In this section, we present the commands to creating a VPC peering connection, accepting a peering request, and adding the appropriate route in your routing table.

1. Create a VPC peering connection between two VPCs with IDs `vpc-9c19a3f4` and `vpc-0214e967`. Record the VPC peering connection ID for further use.

    ```
    $ aws ec2 create-vpc-peering-connection
    --vpc-id vpc-9c19a3f4
    --peer-vpc-id vpc-0214e967
    ```

2. Accept VPC peering connection.

    Here, we will accept the VPC peering connection request with ID `pcx-cf6aa4a6`.

    ```
    $ aws ec2 accept-vpc-peering-connection
    --vpc-peering-connection-id pcx-cf6aa4a6
    ```

3. Add a route in the route table for the VPC peering connection.

    The following command creates the route with the destination CIDR (172.31.16.0/20) and VPC peer connection ID (`pcx-0e6ba567`) in route table `rtb-7f1bda1a`.

    ```
    $ aws ec2 create-route
    ```

```
--route-table-id rtb-7f1bda1a

--destination-cidr-block 172.31.16.0/20

--vpc-peering-connection-id pcx-0e6ba567
```

How it works...

First, we request a VPC peering connection between two VPCs: a requester VPC that we own (that is, `vpc-9c19a3f4`)and a peer VPC with that we want to create a connection (`vpc-0214e967`). Note that the peering connection request expires after 7 days.

In order to activate the VPC peering connection, the owner of the peer VPC must accept the request. In our recipe, as the owner of the peer VPC, we accept the VPC peering connection request. However, note that the owner of the peer VPC may be a person other than you. You can use the `describe-vpc-peering-connections` command to view your outstanding peering connection requests. The VPC peering connection should be in the pending-acceptance state for you to accept the request.

After creating the VPC peering connection, we created a route in our local VPC subnet's route table to direct traffic to the peer VPC. You can also create peering connections between two or more VPCs to provide full access to resources or peer one VPC to access centralized resources. In addition, peering can be implemented between a VPC and specific subnets or instances in one VPC with instances in another VPC. Refer to the Amazon VPC documentation to set up the most appropriate peering connections for your specific requirements.

Connecting on-premise network to VPC using VPN

By following the recipe in this section, you can extend your on-premise data center into the cloud by connecting on-premise network to VPC using VPN. **Internet Protocol Security** (**IPSec**) VPN connections are supported by AWS. You can create both statically routed and dynamically routed VPN connections in a VPC. Virtual private gateway works on the AWS side of the VPN connection and customer gateway (a physical or a software appliance) works on your side of the VPN connection. If you already have an OpenVPN Access Server setup on premises and would like to extend connectivity of your OpenVPN connection to the Amazon Cloud, you can do so easily without purchasing additional hardware. Each VPC connection on the AWS side has two tunnels for redundancy, if one tunnel is taken down for maintenance purposes, your customer gateways can use the second tunnel. Each tunnel has its own unique virtual private gateway public IP address. To handle failures of customer gateways, you can create a second VPN connection using a second customer gateway. After creating a successful VPN connection you have to update your route tables to direct traffic to your on-premise network and update the security groups of the instances and network ACLs of your subnets.

The list of VPN devices that are known to work with Amazon VPC are available at `http://aws.amazon.com/vpc/faqs/#C9`.

How to do it...

In this section, we present the commands for connecting your on-premise network to the VPC using VPN. The steps to accomplish this include creating a customer gateway, a virtual private gateway (and attaching it to your VPC), and static routes for your VPN connection.

1. Create a customer gateway with the `ipsec.1` type. You have to provide the Internet-routable IP address for the customer gateway's external interface. This IP address must be static.

   ```
   $ aws ec2 create-customer-gateway

   --type ipsec.1

   --public-ip 123.252.223.114

   --bgp-asn 65000
   ```

2. Create a virtual private gateway with the `ipsec.1` type.

   ```
   $ aws ec2 create-vpn-gateway

   --type ipsec.1
   ```

3. Attach the virtual private gateway (`vgw-a74f34f5`) to VPC (`vpc-0214e967`).

   ```
   $ aws ec2 attach-vpn-gateway

   --vpn-gateway-id vgw-a74f34f5

   --vpc-id vpc-0214e967
   ```

4. Create a VPN connection with static routing.

   The following command creates the VPN connection with static routing between the customer gateway (`cgw-762b5124`) and virtual private gateway (`vgw-a74f34f5`). The response includes information that you need to give to your network administrator to configure your customer gateway.

   ```
   $ aws ec2 create-vpn-connection

   --type ipsec.1

   --customer-gateway-id cgw-762b5124

   --vpn-gateway-id vgw-a74f34f5

   --options "{\"StaticRoutesOnly\":true}"
   ```

5. Create static routes for the VPN connection (`vpn-d74d3685`). The static route allows traffic to be routed from the virtual private gateway to the VPN customer gateway. You have to prove the CIDR block associated with the local subnet of the customer network.

```
$ aws ec2 create-vpn-connection-route
--vpn-connection-id vpn-d74d3685
--destination-cidr-block 172.30.0.0/16
```

How it works...

First, we create a customer gateway that has information about our VPN device. For doing that, we provided the Internet-routable public IP address of our VPN device. Note that the IP address can't be behind your NAT instance, and it must be static. For dynamic routing, you will need to specify the gateway's **Border Gateway Protocol** (**BGP**) and **Autonomous System Number** (**ASN**); this can be either a public or private ASN (such as those in the 64512–65534 range).

The device on the AWS side of our VPN connection is the virtual private gateway. The virtual private gateway represents the endpoint of our VPN connection. We create a virtual private gateway in our net step. Note that `ipsec.1` is the only supported connection type for this virtual private gateway. Then, we attach the virtual private gateway to our VPC.

In the next step, we create a VPN connection between our virtual private gateway and our customer gateway. We specify the option for static routing, only.

In the final step, we create a static route associated with our VPN connection between the virtual private gateway and the VPN customer gateway. We specify all IP prefixes of our on-premise network in static routing to communicate with instances in your VPC. Any networks not specified here will not be able to communicate with your Amazon instances. For static routing, the static IP prefixes that you specify for your VPN configuration are propagated to the route table after you've created the VPN connection.

After creating your VPN connection, you must test the end-to-end connectivity of your instances. You would typically launch an instance, configure your security group to enable inbound ICMP, and then use ping to test the connection.

It is recommended to set up a second VPN connection for redundancy. This connection can help maintain traffic flows in cases of customer gateway failures and during maintenance on your customer gateway.

3
Managing AWS Resources Using AWS CloudFormation

In this chapter, we will cover recipes for:

- ▸ Creating CloudFormation templates
- ▸ Creating CloudFormation templates from existing AWS resources
- ▸ Deploying applications on EC2 instances
- ▸ Updating a stack

Introduction

In this chapter, we present recipes for using AWS CloudFormation to create, update, and delete a collection of related AWS resources. We use CloudFormation templates to define AWS resources, and any other dependencies and parameters that are required to run a given specific application. A template is essentially a **JavaScript Object Notation** (**JSON**) file. Using AWS CloudFormation, you can implement version control for your infrastructure and define new templates, or use existing ones, to create a stack (a running instance of your template). If the stack creation process fails, then the entire process gets rolled back.

 AWS CloudFormation is provided as a free service, you need to only pay for the AWS resources created.

Creating CloudFormation templates

In this section, we present the recipe to create an AWS CloudFormation template to specify the AWS resources (and their properties). AWS CloudFormation provides editors to help you to edit your CloudFormation templates. These editors are available for both Visual Studio (AWS Toolkit for Visual Studio) and Eclipse (AWS Toolkit for Eclipse) environments. Based on your application-specific requirements, you will need to define parameters, mappings, resources, and output in the template. Image ID, instance type, VPC ID, subnet IDs, a name for the instance, and key/pair names are the required parameters to run this recipe. You can store this template file in a local folder or in S3 storage. Before creating the stack from the template, you should validate the template using CLI.

 You can find sample templates at `http://aws.amazon.com/cloudformation/aws-cloudformation-templates/`.

How to do it...

Here, we present the specific commands to use for defining, validating, and then creating an AWS cloud stack. As an example, we will be creating the CloudFormation template for an autoscaled web application. This application scenario will require us to define an **Elastic Load Balancer** (**ELB**), launching configurations, and autoscaling groups, cloud watch alarms, and security groups. We will also include commands to retrieve the AWS resource descriptions, get access to the stack events, and send event notifications to an SNS topic. Create the stack by performing the following steps:

1. Create a template file (let's name the file `webserverautoscaling.json`) with the JSON string specified as follows:

```
{
  "AWSTemplateFormatVersion" : "2010-09-09",
  "Description" : "AWS CloudFormation template for web
  server auto scaling deployment.",
  "Parameters" : {
    "ImageId" : {
      "Description" : "AMI id.",
      "Type" : "String",
      "Default" : "ami-1e604a4c"
    },
    "InstanceType" : {
      "Description" : "Tomcat EC2 instance type.",
      "Type" : "String",
      "Default" : "m3.medium",
```

```
      "AllowedValues" : ["t2.small", "t2.medium",
      "m1.small", "m1.medium", "m3.medium","m3.large"]
    },
    "VpcId" : {
        "Type" : "String",
        "Description" : "VPC id.",
        "Default" : "vpc-0214e967"
    },
    "Subnets" : {
      "Type" : "CommaDelimitedList",
      "Default" : "subnet-0240b575,subnet-5314c936",
      "Description" : "Subnet id's list."
    },
    "KeyPairName" : {
      "Description" : "EC2 Key Pair to allow SSH access to
      the instances.",
      "Type" : "String",
      "Default" : "ApacheServerKeyPair"
    },
    "NameForNewInstances" : {
      "Description" : "Name for the instances creating in
      Auto Scaling Group.",
      "Type" : "String",
      "Default" : "apacheserver-asg-instance"
    }
  },

  "Mappings" : {

  },

  "Resources" : {
    "SecurityGroup": {
        "Type": "AWS::EC2::SecurityGroup",
        "Properties": {
            "GroupDescription": "Enable port 80 access from
            anywhere.",
            "VpcId" : { "Ref" : "VpcId" },
            "SecurityGroupIngress": [{
                                    "IpProtocol": "tcp",
                                    "FromPort": "80" ,
                                    "ToPort": "80" ,
                                    "CidrIp" : "0.0.0.0/0"
                                    }]
```

```
            }
        },
        "ElasticLoadBalancer" : {
            "Type" : "AWS::ElasticLoadBalancing::LoadBalancer",
            "Properties" : {
                "Subnets" : { "Ref" : "Subnets" },
                "SecurityGroups" : [ { "Ref" : "SecurityGroup"
                } ],
                "Listeners" : [ {
                    "LoadBalancerPort" : "80",
                    "InstancePort" : "80" ,
                    "Protocol" : "HTTP"
                }],
                "HealthCheck" : {
                    "Target" : "HTTP:80/",
                    "HealthyThreshold" : "3",
                    "UnhealthyThreshold" : "5",
                    "Interval" : "30",
                    "Timeout" : "5"
                }
            }
        },
        "WebServerAutoScalingGroup" : {
          "Type" : "AWS::AutoScaling::AutoScalingGroup",
          "Properties" : {
            "AvailabilityZones" : { "Fn::GetAZs" : "" },
            "VPCZoneIdentifier" : { "Ref" : "Subnets" },
            "LaunchConfigurationName" : { "Ref" :
            "LaunchConfig" },
            "MinSize" : "1",
            "MaxSize" : "4",
            "LoadBalancerNames" : [ { "Ref" :
            "ElasticLoadBalancer" } ],
            "HealthCheckGracePeriod" : 300,
            "HealthCheckType" : "ELB",
            "Tags" : [{"Key" : "Name", "Value" : { "Ref" :
            "NameForNewInstances" },"PropagateAtLaunch" :
            true}]
          }
        },

        "LaunchConfig" : {
          "Type" : "AWS::AutoScaling::LaunchConfiguration",
          "Properties" : {
```

```
      "KeyName" : { "Ref" : "KeyPairName" },
      "ImageId" : { "Ref" : "ImageId" },
      "InstanceType" : { "Ref" : "InstanceType" },
      "AssociatePublicIpAddress" : true,
      "SecurityGroups" : [ { "Ref" : "SecurityGroup" } ]
    }
  },

  "WebServerScaleUpPolicy" : {
    "Type" : "AWS::AutoScaling::ScalingPolicy",
    "Properties" : {
      "AdjustmentType" : "ChangeInCapacity",
      "AutoScalingGroupName" : { "Ref" :
      "WebServerAutoScalingGroup" },
      "Cooldown" : "60",
      "ScalingAdjustment" : "1"
    }
  },
  "WebServerScaleDownPolicy" : {
    "Type" : "AWS::AutoScaling::ScalingPolicy",
    "Properties" : {
      "AdjustmentType" : "ChangeInCapacity",
      "AutoScalingGroupName" : { "Ref" :
      "WebServerAutoScalingGroup" },
      "Cooldown" : "60",
      "ScalingAdjustment" : "-1"
    }
  },

  "CPUAlarmHigh": {
   "Type": "AWS::CloudWatch::Alarm",
   "Properties": {
      "AlarmDescription": "Scale-up if CPU > 60% for 10
      minutes",
      "MetricName": "CPUUtilization",
      "Namespace": "AWS/EC2",
      "Statistic": "Average",
      "Period": "300",
      "EvaluationPeriods": "2",
      "Threshold": "60",
      "AlarmActions": [ { "Ref": "WebServerScaleUpPolicy"
      } ],
      "Dimensions": [
        {
```

```
                    "Name": "AutoScalingGroupName",
                    "Value": { "Ref": "WebServerAutoScalingGroup" }
                  }
              ],
              "ComparisonOperator": "GreaterThanThreshold"
           }
        },
        "CPUAlarmLow": {
         "Type": "AWS::CloudWatch::Alarm",
         "Properties": {
            "AlarmDescription": "Scale-down if CPU < 60% for 10
            minutes",
            "MetricName": "CPUUtilization",
            "Namespace": "AWS/EC2",
            "Statistic": "Average",
            "Period": "300",
            "EvaluationPeriods": "2",
            "Threshold": "60",
            "AlarmActions": [ { "Ref":
            "WebServerScaleDownPolicy" } ],
            "Dimensions": [
              {
                "Name": "AutoScalingGroupName",
                "Value": { "Ref": "WebServerAutoScalingGroup" }
              }
            ],
            "ComparisonOperator": "LessThanThreshold"
          }
        }
      },
      "Outputs": {
          "URL": {
              "Value": {
                  "Fn::Join": ["", ["http://", {"Fn::GetAtt":
                  ["ElasticLoadBalancer", "DNSName" ]}]]
              },
              "Description" : "Elastic Load Balancer DNS
               name."
          }
      }
    }
```

2. Validate the template by running the following command to check the syntax of the template:

```
$ aws cloudformation validate-template
--template-body file://F:\\webserverautoscaling.json
```

3. Execute the following command to create a stack called `webserverautoscaling` using the `webserverautoscaling.json` file:

```
$ aws cloudformation create-stack
--stack-name webserverautoscaling
--template-body file://F:\\ webserverautoscaling.json
--parameters ParameterKey=NameForNewInstances,ParameterValue=apach
eserver-asg-pr-instance
```

4. Execute the following command to get all the resources descriptions for the the stack:

```
$ aws cloudformation describe-stack-resources
--stack-name webserverautoscaling
```

5. Execute the following command to get the list of events for the stack:

```
$ aws cloudformation describe-stack-events
--stack-name webserverautoscaling
```

How it works...

In the first step for creating a stack, we use a JSON-based template to declaratively specify the required AWS resources and their properties. In addition, we can also specify the dependencies between the resources, for example, we may want the instances to come up after the load balancer. We also use the template to specify data flows between the resources, for example, passing the database connection strings to the instances.

A template is divided into multiple sections—resources, parameters, mappings, and outputs. The resources section contains the list of all the resources and their specific properties required for the application. These include EC2 instances, RDS databases, security groups, and many more. The parameters section helps you specify the parameters that can be customized at the stack creation time. The parameter section in the template can help you set appropriate values for different environments, for example, you may want to have different number of instances for your test and production stacks, or you may choose to disable the **Multi-AZ** parameter for the RDS service in your testing environment. The mappings section allows you to perform conditional setting of properties, for example, you may want to have region-specific values for the properties. The final section is the outputs section. This section is used to return important data to the user based on the resources created. For example, we may want to pass the URL for a newly created website to the user. The output values get shown in the console.

We set the version number and provide a simple description for our template. In addition, we declaratively define the image, instance types, VPC, subnets, and so on, in the parameters section. For example, for the `InstanceType` parameter, we have a description for the parameter, the data type of the parameter is a string, the default value is `m3.medium`, and the allowed values for the parameter are specified as a list of instance types allowed.

Mappings in templates are like switch statements. Using the `Fn::FindInMap` function, you can get the values from the mappings by giving the key as input. We have not specified any mappings in our example. However, this section can be used to define mappings between region names and specific AMI IDs. For example, the region could be the one where the CloudFromation template is being executed. This region information can be referenced through a `AWS::Region` pseudo-parameter. The `Fn::FindInMap` function will then use the region name to get the appropriate AMI ID.

The AWS resources are defined in the resource section of the CloudFormation template. You can add one or more properties to the specified resources. Each resource has a logical name that you can use to reference the resource in the template. We have also declared an IAM security group, ELB, launch configuration, autoscaling group, and CloudWatch alarm resources. Each resource has its own set of properties to be specified. For example, in the case of the security group resource, we specify the type of resource and the ingress rules. We use the `Ref` function at several places, as we do not know the physical ID of the resource that will be created. This function will return the value of the property based on the actual physical ID of the resource that is created. The CloudFormation service displays the actual values of the resources as specified in the outputs section in the template after the stack is successfully created. We use the `Join` function to concatenate strings. Here, we concatenate the `http://` string with the DNS name. The DNS name is retrieved using the `GetAtt` function on the appropriate resource.

In the next step, we validate the template, which includes checks for structure and API usage, JSON syntax, presence of circular dependencies, and so on. Validating the template can help save you a lot of time. However, if AWS CloudFormation fails to create the stack, then you can use the CloudFormation console to view the failure event and understand the reason for it. For debugging EC2 provisioning failures, you can view the `cloud-init` and `cfn` logs, or publish these logs to CloudWatch and view them in the AWS Management Console.

After creating and validating the template, you have to provide the template file path to the `create-stack` command to create the stack using the specified template. While creating the stack, we can pass specific parameters in the parameters section, for example, `apacheserver-asg-pr-instance` is the autoscaling group for our production environment.

The next command is very helpful in verifying the stack you just created. The response of the `describe-stack` command includes the stack name and ID, resource names, physical IDs, resource types, current status of the resources, and the descriptions of the resources. Finally, we execute the `describe-stack-events` command to retrieve all the stack-related events for our stack.

There's more...

Instead of executing the `create-stack` command, as specified in step 4, you can execute the following command to sends the stack event notifications to a **Simple Notification Service (SNS)** topic. Execute the following command to send the stack event notifications to a SNS topic called `Test`.

```
$ aws cloudformation create-stack

--stack-name webserverautoscaling

--template-body file://F:\\ webserverautoscaling.json

--parameters ParameterKey=NameForNewInstances,ParameterValue=apacheserv
er-asg-pr-instance

--notification-arns

"arn:aws:sns:ap-southeast-1:968336292411:Test"
```

Before running this command, you will need to create an SNS topic called `Test`. You can subscribe to this topic to receive e-mail notifications.

Creating CloudFormation templates from existing AWS resources

AWS CloudFormer can be used to create AWS CloudFormation templates from the existing AWS resources. This section describes the steps for creating a CloudFormation template from your existing AWS resources using the CloudFormer tool. The AWS CloudFormer tool will automatically detect the dependent resources for a given AWS resource. For example, if you select an EC2 instance, then CloudFormer will automatically select the associated security groups.

How to do it...

Follow the steps to create your AWS CloudFormation template from your existing AWS resources:

1. Login to the AWS console.
2. Navigate to the CloudFormation service.
3. Click on **Launch CloudFormer** and continue with default options. If you want to restrict the access to CloudFormation tool, specify the appropriate IP address range. Check the checkbox that says **I acknowledge that this template might cause AWS CloudFormation to create IAM resources**.
4. Within minutes, your CloudFormer stack will be created. Get the URL for your CloudFormer tool in the outputs section.

5. After navigating to the tool, select the AWS region from the **Select the AWS Region** drop-down box.

6. After selecting the region, click on the **Create Template** button. This will analyze all the AWS resources in your account.

7. After analyzing AWS resources in your account, the CloudFormer tool displays an interface to select the DNS (Route53), VPC, VPC network (subnets, Internet gateways, customer gateways, DHCP options, VPN connections), VPC security (network ACLs, route tables), network (ELB, EIP, network interfaces, CloudFront distributions), compute (autoscaling groups, EC2 instances), storage (EBS volumes, RDS databases instances, DynamoDB tables, S3 buckets), services (Elastic Cache Clusters, SQS queues, SNS topics, SimpleDB domains), config (autoscaling launch configurations, RDS DB subnet groups, RDS DB parameter groups, Elastic Cache Parameter groups), security (EC2 security groups, RDS security groups, Elastic Cache Security groups, SQS queue policies, S3 bucket policies, operational (autoscaling policies, CloudWatch alarms). Select the required AWS resources in your AWS account.

8. After verifying the template, you can save the template in an S3 bucket.

9. Using this CloudFormation template, you can recreate your infrastructure.

10. After creating the CloudFormer template, remember to delete the CloudFormer stack to avoid additional billing.

How it works...

AWS CloudFormer is itself a CloudFormation stack, so we need to launch it. As a result of launching the stack, a `t1.micro` EC2 instance is created, automatically, and the URL is displayed in the output section. We access the URL to get access to the CloudFormer tool. CloudFormer helps you create a template from your running resources. It runs through all the resources in your account, and then lets you select the resources you want to include in your template. In addition, you can customize the names and define new outputs. CloudFormer will fill in the values for various properties in the starter template, for example, the Availability Zone for an EC2 instance. You will need to edit the starter template to include additional parameters or abstract away various properties. After generating the CloudFormation templates from the existing AWS resources, you can delete the CloudFormer stack to avoid additional billing for the `t1.micro` EC2 instance.

Deploying applications on EC2 instances

You can deploy your applications on EC2 instances using AWS CloudFormation. In this AWS CloudFormation template, for example, we will install an Apache server and deploy code to it. We also create EIP, SecurityGroup, and EC2 resources. Image ID, instance type, VPC ID, subnet ID, a name for the instance, and key/pair names are required parameters to run this recipe. As this is a public facing web application, use the public subnet in your VPC.

How to do it...

Follow the steps to install an Apache server and deploy some code to it:

1. Create the CloudFormation template file JSON file (named
   apachewebserverdeployment.json) with the following content:

```json
{
  "AWSTemplateFormatVersion" : "2010-09-09",
  "Description" : "AWS CloudFormation template for Apache
  Server.",
  "Parameters" : {
    "ImageId" : {
      "Description" : "AMI Id.",
      "Type" : "String",
      "Default" : "ami-7e2c612c"
    },
    "InstanceType" : {
      "Description" : "Tomcat EC2 instance type.",
      "Type" : "String",
      "Default" : "m3.medium",
      "AllowedValues" : ["t2.small", "t2.medium",
      "m1.small", "m1.medium", "m3.medium","m3.large"]
    },
    "VpcId" : {
        "Type" : "String",
        "Description" : "VPC Id.",
        "Default" : "vpc-0214e967"
    },
    "Subnet" : {
      "Type" : "String",
      "Default" : "subnet-0240b575",
      "Description" : "Subnet Id."
    },
    "KeyPairName" : {
      "Description" : "EC2 Key Pair to allow SSH access to
      the instances.",
      "Type" : "String",
      "Default" : "ApacheServerKeyPair"
    },
    "InstanceName" : {
      "Description" : "Name for the instance.",
      "Type" : "String",
      "Default" : "apacheserver-01"
```

```
        }
      },

      "Mappings" : {

      },

      "Resources" : {
        "ApacheServer" : {
            "Type" : "AWS::EC2::Instance",
            "Metadata" : {
               "Comment" : "Deploy HTML application to Apache
               Web Server",
               "AWS::CloudFormation::Init" : {
                    "config" : {
                        "packages" : {
                            "apt" : {
                                "apache2" : []
                            }
                        },
                        "sources" : {
                          "/var/www/" : "https://s3-ap-
                          southeast-1.amazonaws.com/c3htmlapp
                          /application.zip"
                        },
                        "services" : {
                            "sysvinit" : {
                                "apache2"     : { "enabled" :
                                "true", "ensureRunning" :
                                "true" }
                            }
                        }
                    }
                }
            },
             "Properties" : {
                "UserData": {"Fn::Base64": {"Fn::Join": ["", [
                    "#!/bin/bash\n",
                    "sudo apt-get update\n",
                    "sudo apt-get -y install python-setuptools
                    python-pip\n",
                    "sudo easy_install
                    https://s3.amazonaws.com/cloudformation-
                    examples/aws-cfn-bootstrap-
                    latest.tar.gz\n",
```

```
                        "sudo /usr/local/bin/cfn-init -s ",
                        { "Ref" : "AWS::StackName" },
                        "     -r ApacheServer",
                        "     --region ",
                        { "Ref" : "AWS::Region" },
                        "\n"
            ]]}},
            "ImageId" : { "Ref" : "ImageId" },
            "KeyName" : { "Ref" : "KeyPairName" },
            "SecurityGroupIds" : [{ "Ref" : "SecurityGroup"
             }],
            "InstanceType" : { "Ref" : "InstanceType" },
            "SubnetId" : { "Ref" : "Subnet" },
            "Tags" : [ {"Key" : "Name", "Value" : { "Ref" :
            "InstanceName"} } ]
        }
    },
    "IPAddress" : {
      "Type" : "AWS::EC2::EIP",
      "Properties" : {
        "Domain" : "vpc",
        "InstanceId" : { "Ref" : "ApacheServer" }
      }
    },
    "SecurityGroup": {
        "Type": "AWS::EC2::SecurityGroup",
        "Properties": {
            "GroupDescription": "Enable port 80 access from
              anywhere.",
            "VpcId" : { "Ref" : "VpcId" },
            "SecurityGroupIngress": [{
                                        "IpProtocol": "tcp",
                                        "FromPort": "80" ,
                                        "ToPort": "80" ,
                                        "CidrIp" : "0.0.0.0/0"
                                        },
                                        {
                                        "IpProtocol": "tcp",
                                        "FromPort": "22" ,
                                        "ToPort": "22" ,
                                        "CidrIp" : "0.0.0.0/0"
                                        }]
                    }
    }
}
```

```
        },

        "Outputs": {
                "URL": {
                        "Value": {
                                "Fn::Join": ["", ["http://",
                                {"Fn::GetAtt": ["ApacheServer",
                                "PublicIp" ]}]]
                        },
                        "Description" : "Apache Server Public Ip
                                        Address."

                }
        }
}
```

2. Execute the following command to create the stack using the preceding CloudFormation template specified:

```
$ aws cloudformation create-stack

--stack-name apachewebserverdeployment

--template-body file://F:\\apachewebserverdeployment.json

--parameters ParameterKey=InstanceName,ParameterValue=apacheserv
er-pr-01
```

How it works...

In the first step for creating a stack, we use a JSON-based template to declaratively specify the required AWS resources and their properties. In addition, we can also specify the dependencies between the resources, for example, we may want the instances to come up after the load balancer. We also use the template to specify data flows between the resources, for example, passing the database connection strings to the instances.

A template is divided into multiple sections—resources, parameters, mappings, and outputs. The resources section contains the list of all the resources and their specific properties required for the application. These include EC2 instances, RDS databases, security groups, and so on. The parameters section helps you specify the parameters that can be customized at the stack creation time. The parameter section in the template can help you set appropriate values for different environments, for example, you may want to have different number of instances for your test and production stacks, or you may choose to disable the **Multi-AZ** parameter for the RDS service in your testing environment. The mappings section allows you to do conditional setting of properties, for example, you may want to have region-specific values for the properties. The final section is the outputs section. This section is used to return important data to the user, based on the resources created. For example, we may want to pass the URL for a newly created website to the user. The output values get shown in the console.

We set the version number and provide a simple description for our template. In addition, we declaratively define the image, instance types, VPC, subnets, and so on in the parameters section. For example, for the `InstanceType` parameter, we have a description for the parameter, the data type of the parameter is a string, the default value is `m3.medium`, and the allowed values for the parameter are specified as a list of instance types allowed.

Mappings in templates are like switch statements. Using the `Fn::FindInMap` function, you can get the values from the mappings by giving the key as input. We have not specified any mappings in our example. However, this section can be used to define mappings between region names and specific AMI IDs. For example, the region could be the one where the CloudFromation template is being executed. This region information can be referenced through a `AWS::Region` pseudo parameter. The `Fn::FindInMap` function will then use the region name to get the appropriate AMI ID.

The AWS resources are defined in the resource section of the CloudFormation template. You can add one or more properties to the specified resources. Each resource has a logical name that you can use to reference the resource in the template. We have also declared an **Elastic IP** (**EIP**) address and an IAM security group. The IPAddress resource associates an EIP with the instance. Each resource has its own set of properties to be specified. For example, in case of the security group resource we specify, the type of resource and the ingress rules.

As we want to download and install our application on our instance, we can use a set of CloudFormation helper functions. These are functions that run on the instance to pull down the files, packages, and so on, need to run on the instance as it starts up. These functions are installed by default on Amazon Linux and Windows AMIs. You can complete the following tasks using the Cloudformation helper functions:

1. Create files, groups, and users.
2. Install packages and services.
3. Get source code from your source control system.

Metadata defined in the `AWS::CloudFormation::Init` key, which is then read by the `cfn-init` helper script. The config section is used to specify packages, files to pull down, services to start, and so on. In this recipe, we specify the download and installation of Apache web server (when the instance starts up) in the packages subsection. In the sources subsection, we specify the location of the ZIP file we want to pull from S3 storage and where to put it (`/var/www`). In the services subsection, we specify the startup of the Apache daemon and ensure that it is enabled and running.

The `UserData` property of EC2 instance complete the listed tasks:

1. Update the `aptcache`.
2. Install PHP tools.
3. Install CloudFormation helper scripts using `easy_install` tools.

4. Run the `cfn-init` scripts. When you run the `cfn-init` script, it reads metadata from `AWS::CloudFormation::Init` property, installs the `apache2` server, downloads the code from the S3 bucket, and copies it to the `/var/www/` folder. It will also ensure that the Apache server will be started automatically upon boot.

The output of the preceding CloudFormation template is the EIP address of EC2 instance. Apache server installation and code retrieval from the S3 bucket can take time. By default, CloudFormation shows stack complete status after all the resources have been created. Instead, if you want to wait for the installation and configuration on EC2 instances to be fully completed, then you have to create `CreationPolicy` on the EC2 resource and send success signals after the installation and configuration is completed.

We use the `Ref` function at several places, as we do not know the physical ID of the resource that will be created. This function will return the value of the property based on the actual physical ID of the resource that is created. The CloudFormation service displays the actual values of the resources as specified in the outputs section in the template after the stack is successfully created. We use the `Join` function to concatenate strings. Here, we concatenate the `http://` string with the public IP address. The IP address is retrieved using the `GetAtt` function on the appropriate resource.

Updating a stack

When you update a stack using AWS CloudFormation, it compares the current version of the template with the previous one and then updates the AWS resources accordingly. You can specify stack policies to avoid accidental updates to your AWS resources. You can also use a single stack policy to specify the restrictions for multiple resources. However, you can only apply one stack policy for the stack at any given time. Stack policies are specified in the JSON format. If you don't specify a stack policy for your stack then, by default, you will be able to update any of the resources. Also, if a stack policy is specified, then, by default, it will restrict all updates unless you explicitly specify `Allow` statements for your resources.

How to do it...

Follow these steps to update your stack:

1. Create a stack policy as a JSON file (name it `webserverautoscalingpolicy.json`) with the following content:

```
{
"Statement" : [
{
"Effect" : "Deny",
"Action" : "Update:*",
"Principal": "*",
```

```
"Resource" : "LogicalResourceId/SecurityGroup"
},
{
"Effect" : "Allow",
"Action" : "Update:*",
"Principal": "*",
"Resource" : "*"
}
]
}
```

2. Associate the preceding policy with your stack using the following command:

   ```
   $ aws cloudformation set-stack-policy
   --stack-name webserverautoscaling
   --stack-policy-body
   file://F:\\webserverautoscalingpolicy.json
   ```

3. After applying the preceding policy, if you update your stack by changing your SecurityGroup resource in the template, you will get an error. You can update stack by executing the following command:

   ```
   $ aws cloudformation update-stack
   --stack-name webserverautoscaling
   --template-body file://F:\\webserverautoscaling.json
   ```

How it works...

You can update your stack in response to evolving requirements of your application. These updates can include properties of existing resources, adding and/or removing resources, and updating the software running on your instances. These are typically achieved by making changes to your template file. When you submit an updated template, AWS CloudFormation updates the resources based on the differences between your currently running stack and the updated template. Certain updates can be made without interruptions, while others may require your resources to be replaced. In order to restrict modifications, you use the Effect parameter in your stack policy.

The Effect parameter in the policy is for allowing or denying actions to the security group. Update actions are either Allowed or Denied. These include the Update:Modify, Update:Replace, Update:Delete, Update:* options. You can explicitly specify multiple update actions or use regular expression such as Update:* to denote all update actions. If you want to exclude some update actions, you can use NotAction. Here we are denying the all update actions. You will need to specify the logical IDs of the resources to which the policy applies. You can also use regular expressions for this purpose. If you want to exclude some resources you can use NotResource.

In the next step, we set the stack policy to the `webserverautoscaling` stack. At this stage, if you try to update the stack you will get an error. In the final step, we run the command to update the stack.

Downloading the example code
You can download the example code files from your account at `http://www.packtpub.com` for all the Packt Publishing books you have purchased. If you purchased this book elsewhere, you can visit `http://www.packtpub.com/support` and register to have the files e-mailed directly to you.

4

Securing Access to Amazon EC2 Instances

In this chapter, we will cover recipes for:

- ▶ Creating IAM users
- ▶ Creating IAM groups and assigning group-level permissions
- ▶ Creating IAM roles
- ▶ Connecting on-premise AD to AWS IAM
- ▶ Configuring AWS multifactor authentication

Introduction

AWS Identity and Access Management (**IAM**) enables centralized control to secure access to AWS services and resources for your users. Using IAM, you can create and manage AWS users and groups, and use fine-grained permissions to allow and deny their access to AWS resources.

In this chapter, we present recipes for using AWS IAM to create users and roles, and assign appropriate permissions to securely access AWS services. Users can also be added to a group using the IAM groups feature and permissions can be assigned at the group level. You can integrate your on-premise active directory with IAM. You can also assign policies to users, groups, and roles where the policies contain one or more permissions. Finally, we present a recipe to configure multifactor authentication (for enhanced security) to access certain AWS services.

Creating IAM users

As a best practice, you should create individual users rather than share your credentials to be used by other users. This ensures that you create unique users with their own individual credentials. In addition, this allows you to rotate individual credentials and assign users individual permissions. Typically, you would identify the IAM users in your organization, create their credentials, and assign suitable permissions to them.

You can create IAM users using AWS console, API or CLI. After creating an IAM user, you need to configure the password, access keys, and MFA devices for that user. By default, a new user created in IAM does not have any permission, that is, the user exists but does not have access to any of the services. To assign permissions to the user, you will have to create a policy. The policy is a JSON document that contains one or more permissions. You can use predefined policy templates or use the policy generator.

How to do it...

1. Create an IAM user.

   Execute the following command to create a user named `ethanhunt`:

   ```
   $ aws iam create-user
   --user-name ethanhunt
   ```

2. Set the password for IAM user.

   Execute the following command to set a new password for the user:

   ```
   $ aws iam create-login-profile
   --user-name ethanhunt
   --password P@ssw0rd
   ```

3. Create an inline IAM policy for the user.

   Create a new JSON file with the contents listed and save the file as `S3ReadAccess.json`. The following sample policy gives permissions to list all the `S3buckets`, and to list, upload, get, and delete objects in the bucket named `ethanhunt`.

   ```
   {
           "Version": "2012-10-17",
           "Statement": [
           {
               "Effect": "Allow",
               "Action": ["s3:ListAllMyBuckets"],
               "Resource": "arn:aws:s3:::*"
           },
   ```

```
    {
        "Effect": "Allow",
        "Action": [
            "s3:ListBucket",
            "s3:GetBucketLocation"
        ],
        "Resource": "arn:aws:s3:::ethanhunt"
    },
    {

        "Effect": "Allow",
        "Action": [
        "s3:PutObject",
        "s3:GetObject",
        "s3:DeleteObject"
        ],
        "Resource": "arn:aws:s3:::ethanhunt/*"
    }
    ]
}
```

4. Execute the following command to create a policy, S3ReadAccess, using the JSON document (S3ReadAccess.json):

```
$ aws iam put-user-policy
--user-name ethanhunt
--policy-name S3ReadAccess
--policy-document file://F:\\S3ReadAccess.json
```

How it works...

First, we create an IAM user, and then we assign the permissions and the password. As a best practice, we always follow the principle of assigning the least privilege to any given user. For example, if a user doesn't make API calls, then we don't create the access keys for that user. This practice will ensure a more granular control over API and resource usage, and a lesser chance of a user making mistakes. The assigned password is required to log in into the AWS console. Ensure that you store the password in a secure location because if the password is lost, then you can't recover it. In addition, as a best practice reduce or eliminate the use of root account because this account cannot be controlled by IAM policies. Typically, we delete the access keys and assign a MFA device to the account to achieve this.

Policies contain one or more permissions. In our example, upon creation of a new user, we create a policy to assign permissions to the user to be able to access the AWS services (EC2, S3, DynamoDB, and so on.) However, there are policy templates readily available or most scenarios that you can use to customize for your own use.

There are two types of policies—managed and inline. Managed policies can be attached to multiple users, groups, and roles. Inline policies are directly embedded in a user, group, or role definition. In the next step, we create an inline policy and attach it to the user. We need to specify the following parameters in the policy-version, effect (whether the user is allowed to access or not), action (specific actions that are allowed or denied), and resource (identifies the specific AWS resource).

Creating IAM groups and assigning group-level permissions

You can manage users better using IAM groups than by managing them as individual users. Using groups, you can assign same permissions to multiple users. This makes it easier to assign the same permissions to multiple users. In addition, it also becomes simpler to update or reassign permissions for multiple users, or move users between groups.

Typically, you would map permissions to a specific business function in your organization followed by assigning users to that function. After creating groups, you have to create a policy and assign it to the group. Policy variables and groups allow you to manage your users without hardcoding each user in the policy.

How to do it...

1. Create IAM group.

   Execute the following command to create a group called `developers`:

   ```
   $ aws iam create-group
   --group-name developers
   ```

2. Add a user to the group.

   Execute the following command to add the previously created user, `ethanhunt`, to the `developers` group:

   ```
   $ aws iam add-user-to-group
   --user-name ethanhunt
   --group-name developers
   ```

3. Create an inline IAM policy for the group.

Follow these steps to create an inline IAM policy. After creating the policy, you can attach it to the `developers` group.

1. Create a JSON policy document with the following content, and then save the file as `EC2DevGroupPolicy.json`. The first statement allows all users in the `developers` group to list all the EC2 instances, and the second statement allows the users in the `developers` group to terminate instances with the `dev` resource tag. Here, the users in the `developers` group don't have the permission to launch an EC2 instance. In the resource parameter, replace the region name and account number with your own values. To find your AWS account ID number in the AWS Management Console, click on **Support** in the navigation bar in the upper-right corner, and then click on **Support Center**. Your currently signed-in account ID appears below the **Support** menu.

```
{
  "Version": "2012-10-17",
  "Statement": [
    {
      "Effect": "Allow",
      "Action": "ec2:DescribeInstances",
      "Resource": "*"
    },
    {
      "Effect": "Allow",
      "Action": "ec2:TerminateInstances",
      "Resource": "arn:aws:ec2:ap-southeast-
1:968336292411:instance/*",
      "Condition": {
        "StringEquals": {
          "ec2:ResourceTag/stack": "dev"
        }
      }
    }
  ]
}
```

2. Get the list of users in the group using the following command.

```
$ aws iam get-group --group-name developers
```

3. Execute the following command to assign the inline policy to the `developers` group:

```
$ aws iam put-group-policy
--group-name developers
--policy-name EC2DevGroupPolicy
--policy-document file://F:\\EC2DevGroupPolicy.json
```

How it works...

As the first step, we create an IAM group so that we can add users to it. As a best practice, create a group even if you have a single user in it. This helps any future users having the same requirements to be added quickly to the same group. Creating groups also helps in managing a set of users, as users may be added or removed from the group at any time.

You can restrict access further using conditions. Conditions allow for additional granularity in permissions. There are some conditions that are common across AWS services and others that are service specific. However, ensure that you don't overuse conditions, as it can result in a very restrictive environment.

Creating IAM roles

An IAM role is a container for a policy. Using IAM roles for EC2 instances allows for easy management of access keys and for their automatic rotation, that is, Amazon rotates the keys several times a day without requiring any specific action from your end. Hence, you should not have the access keys as a part of the AMI or your application, as their rotation becomes unnecessarily complicated. We just need to create an IAM role, assign permissions to the role, and then launch the EC2 instances to make this work.

After creating a role, you will also need to create a policy and assign it to the newly created role. For example, if an EC2 instance needs access to other AWS services, such as S3 buckets or DynamoDB tables, then you can create a role for it. You will assign the role permissions that allow access to S3/DynamoDB, and finally launch the EC2 instance with that role. You can create one role and attach it to multiple EC2 instances.

How to do it...

1. Create an IAM role for EC2.

   Execute the following commands to create a role for an AWS service. You will need to specify who can assume this role in the JSON document.

   1. Create a new JSON document with the following content and save as S3RoleForEC2.json:

      ```
      {
      "Version": "2012-10-17",
          "Statement": {
              "Effect": "Allow",
              "Principal": {"Service": "ec2.amazonaws.com"},
              "Action": "sts:AssumeRole"
          }
      }
      ```

2. Execute the following command to create the `S3RoleForEC2` role using the JSON document:

```
$ aws iam create-role
--role-name S3RoleForEC2
--assume-role-policy-document
file://F:\\S3RoleForEC2.json
```

2. Create an inline policy for the role.

   After creating a role, you need to assign permissions to it. For example, in our sample policy, we are allowing access to an S3 bucket named `appconfiguration` from the EC2 instance.

   1. Create the JSON document with the following content. We are giving the appropriate permissions to list objects in the bucket, and to put, get, and delete objects from the bucket. Save the file as `S3RoleForEC2Policy.json`.

```
{
    "Version": "2012-10-17",
    "Statement": [
        {
            "Effect": "Allow",
            "Action": [
                "s3:ListBucket"
            ],
            "Resource": "arn:aws:s3:::appconfiguration"
        },
        {
            "Effect": "Allow",
            "Action": [
                "s3:PutObject",
                "s3:GetObject",
                "s3:DeleteObject"
            ],
            "Resource":
            "arn:aws:s3:::appconfiguration/*"
        }
    ]
}
```

   2. Execute the following command to assign the new inline policy to the `S3RoleForEC2` role.

```
$ aws iam put-role-policy
--role-name S3RoleForEC2
```

```
--policy-name S3RoleForEC2Policy
--policy-document
file://F:\\S3RoleForEC2Policy.json
```

3. Create and assign an instance profile to the role.

    Execute the following commands to first create an instance profile, and then add the role to the instance profile.

    1. Create an instance profile.

        Execute the following command to create an instance profile named S3RoleForEC2Profile:

        ```
        $ aws iam create-instance-profile
        --instance-profile-name S3RoleForEC2Profile
        ```

    2. Add the role to the instance profile.

    3. The following command adds the role named S3RoleForEC2 to the instance profile named S3RoleForEC2Profile.

        ```
        $ aws iam add-role-to-instance-profile
        --instance-profile-name S3RoleForEC2Profile
        --role-name S3RoleForEC2
        ```

4. Launch an EC2 instance with the role.

    After creating the role you can launch your EC2 instance with IAM roles. Execute the following command to create the EC2 instance with the instance profile created earlier. Before executing the command, you should have already created the key pairs, security groups, VPC, and subnet.

    ```
    $ aws ec2 run-instances
    --image-id ami-7e2c612c
    --count 1
    --instance-type t2.micro
    --key-name MyKeyPair
    --security-group-ids sg-ad70b8c8
    --subnet-id subnet-aed11acb
    --iam-instance-profile Name=S3RoleForEC2Profile
    ```

5. Test the installation.

    Execute the following command to get the list of objects in the appconfiguration bucket:

    ```
    s3 ls s3://appconfiguration/
    ```

If you try to access other buckets, you should get an access denied message. In addition, test uploading and deleting files in the appconfiguration bucket from your EC2 instance.

How it works...

As a first step, we create an IAM role. In order to do that, we create a policy containing the requisite permissions and specify the policy in the create role command. If you use the AWS console for creating role, AWS automatically creates the instance profile with same name as role. But if you a create role from command line, you have to create the instance profile yourself. Hence, we create an instance profile and add the role to it. You have to provide both role name and instance profile name. Finally, we launch the instance specifying the image, number of instances to create, type of EC2 instances, key/pair name, security group IDs, and the subnet, as a good practice test and verify the installation.

Following a least privilege approach, we would typically create and assign roles to provide appropriate access to an application running on an EC2 instance rather than to the instance itself.

There's more...

Roles are also used to share access without sharing the actual access credentials. This is particularly useful for giving a user temporary access to perform a task and in cases where you want to provide cross-account access. For example, if you have separate AWS dev and prod accounts, then you can use roles to give your dev users temporary credentials to access the prod environment.

In order to implement these use cases, you need to create a new role and use policies to specify who can assume this role and what they can do (after they assumed this role). After the role is created, you just need to share the role name and the account ID with the user. For example, if you want to give a specific developer belonging to the dev account read access to an RDB database in the production account. For this, you will need to define a new role name and specify in the policy that IAM users from your dev account are allowed read-only access to the resource. The developer's access policy (in the dev account) is also changed to allow him/her to assume the newly defined role in the production account. When developer requests access to the production database using his/her own credentials, and receives a set of temporary credentials to enable the access to the production database.

Connecting on-premise AD to AWS IAM

You can access AWS services using your corporate credentials as defined in your existing **Active Directory Federation Services** (**ADFS**) setup. You can also integrate AWS with ADFS to implement single sign-on functionality. When using ADFS with AWS, ADFS acts as the identity provider and AWS acts as a relying party. This recipe includes commands and instructions to create a proxy server to get the temporary credentials from AWS **Security Token Service** (**STS**) and a client application that accesses an S3 bucket (using the temporary credentials) from a C# application.

How to do it...

1. Create a proxy application.

    Create a simple **Windows Communication Foundation** (**WCF**) application and add
    a WCF service class. WCF is a framework for building service-oriented applications.
    Using WCF, you can send data as asynchronous messages from one service endpoint
    to another. A service endpoint can be a part of continuously available service hosted
    by IIS, or it can be a service hosted in an application. In the class, create a Get
    method that calls STS service for the temporary credentials.

```
TemporaryCredentials IProxyService.GetToken()
{
//Get username from client request.
string userName =
HttpContext.Current.Request.LogonUserIdentity.Name;

TemporaryCredentials objTemporaryCredentials = new
TemporaryCredentials();

//Get the app settings from web.config file.
NameValueCollection appConfig =
ConfigurationManager.AppSettings;
string accessKeyId = appConfig["accessKeyId"];
string secretAccessKey = appConfig["secretAccessKey"];
string bucketName = appConfig["bucketName"];

// Create a client.
AmazonSecurityTokenServiceConfig config = new
AmazonSecurityTokenServiceConfig();
AmazonSecurityTokenServiceClient client = new
AmazonSecurityTokenServiceClient(
accessKeyId,
secretAccessKey,
config);

//Split the user name.
string[] usernameParts01 = userName.Split('\\');

// Build the aws username.
string awsUsernameDomain = usernameParts01[1] + "@" +
usernameParts01[0];

// Split username@domain to retrieve the username only.
string[] usernameParts02 = awsUsernameDomain.Split('@');
```

```
//Get username only.
string awsUsername = usernameParts02[0];

string policy = appConfig["policy_" + awsUsername];

// Replace the [*] values with real values at runtime.
policy = policy.Replace("[BUCKET-NAME]", bucketName);
policy = policy.Replace("[USER-NAME]",
awsUsername.ToLowerInvariant());
policy = policy.Replace("'", "\"");

//Request to get temporary credentials.
GetFederationTokenRequest request = new
GetFederationTokenRequest
{
DurationSeconds = 3600 * 8,
Name = awsUsername,
Policy = policy
};

//Get temporary credentials.
GetFederationTokenResponse objGetFederationTokenResponse =
client.GetFederationToken(request);

//Get federation token result.
GetFederationTokenResult objGetFederationTokenResult =
objGetFederationTokenResponse.GetFederationTokenResult;

//Get credentials.
Credentials objCredentials =
objGetFederationTokenResult.Credentials;

//Set user name.
objTemporaryCredentials.User = userName;

//Set access key id.
objTemporaryCredentials.AccessKeyId =
objCredentials.AccessKeyId;

//Set secret access key.
objTemporaryCredentials.SecretAccessKey =
objCredentials.SecretAccessKey;

//Set expiration.
```

```
objTemporaryCredentials.Expiration =
objCredentials.Expiration;

//Set token.
objTemporaryCredentials.Token =
objCredentials.SessionToken;

//Return result.
return objTemporaryCredentials;
}
```

2. Create a policy in the app settings section with the `policy_username` key.

   Using policy file specified, the user can list objects in the specified bucket and get objects from the folder with his name:

```
{
'Statement':
[
{
'Sid': 'PersonalBucketAccess',
        'Action': [ 's3:GetObject' ],
        'Effect': 'Allow',
        'Resource': 'arn:aws:s3:::[BUCKET-NAME]/[USER-
        NAME]/*'
},
{
        'Sid': 'GeneralBucketList',
        'Action': [ 's3:ListBucket' ],
        'Effect': 'Allow',
'Resource': 'arn:aws:s3:::[BUCKET-NAME]'
}
]
}
```

3. Host the WCF service and set the authentication to **Windows Authentication** for this application on IIS. You will need to add the following binding configuration in your `web.config` file. The configuration sets the security mode to `TransportCredentialOnly`.

```
<bindings>
<webHttpBinding>
<binding name="default">
  <security mode="TransportCredentialOnly">
    <transport clientCredentialType="Windows"
    proxyCredentialType="Windows" />
  </security>
```

```
    </binding>
    </webHttpBinding>
    </bindings>
```

4. Create a client application.

    Create a C# console application that accomplishes the following tasks:

    ❏   Call the proxy server and get temporary credentials

    ❏   Get list of object in the specified bucket

    ❏   Get file data from the specified bucket

    If you try to access the folder belonging to a user other than the logged-in user, you will get an *access denied* message.

```csharp
//Web request to call proxy service.
HttpWebRequest request =
(HttpWebRequest)WebRequest.Create("
http://ProxyServiceURL/ProxyService.svc/GetToken ");

request.UseDefaultCredentials = true;
request.Credentials =
System.Net.CredentialCache.DefaultCredentials;

//Get the response.
HttpWebResponse response = response = (HttpWebResponse)request.
GetResponse();

//Check for status code.
if (response.StatusCode == HttpStatusCode.OK)
            {
//Get response stream.
using (StreamReader reader = new
StreamReader(response.GetResponseStream()))
                {
//Read response.
                string json = reader.ReadToEnd();

//Initialize DataContractJsonSerializer.
                DataContractJsonSerializer serializer =
                new
                DataContractJsonSerializer
                (typeof(TemporaryCredentials));

    //Get memory stream.
```

```
                    MemoryStream ms = new
                    MemoryStream
                    (Encoding.Default.GetBytes(json));

//Get deserialized object.
                    TemporaryCredentials
                    objTemporaryCredentials =
                    (TemporaryCredentials)
                    serializer.ReadObject(ms);

//Bucket name.
                    string bucketName = "clientdocs01";

//File name.
                    string fileName =
                    "administrator/Note.txt";

//Set AWS credentials and token.
                    SessionAWSCredentials
                    objSessionAWSCredentials = new
                    SessionAWSCredentials(
                    objTemporaryCredentials.AccessKeyId,
                    objTemporaryCredentials.SecretAccessKey,
                    objTemporaryCredentials.Token);

//Create S3 client object to access S3 service.
                    AmazonS3Client objAmazonS3Client = new
                    AmazonS3Client(objSessionAWSCredentials,
                    Amazon.RegionEndpoint.APSoutheast1);

//Prepare list object request.
                    ListObjectsRequest
                    objListObjectsRequest = new
                    ListObjectsRequest();

//Set bucket name.
                    objListObjectsRequest.BucketName =
                    bucketName;

//Get response from AWS S3.
                    ListObjectsResponse
                    objListObjectsResponse =
                    objAmazonS3Client.ListObjects
                    (objListObjectsRequest);
```

```
//Iterate over S3 objects.
            for (int i = 0; i <
            objListObjectsResponse.S3Objects.Count;
             i++)
            {
//Display object name.
                Console.WriteLine("\t" +
                objListObjectsResponse.
                S3Objects[i].Key);
            }

//Prepare get object request.
            GetObjectRequest objGetObjectRequest =
            new GetObjectRequest();

//Set bucket name.
            objGetObjectRequest.BucketName =
            bucketName;

//Set file name.
            objGetObjectRequest.Key = fileName;

//Get object data.
            GetObjectResponse objGetObjectResponse
            = objAmazonS3Client.GetObject
            (objGetObjectRequest);

//Get response stream.
            using (StreamReader objStreamReader =
            new StreamReader
            (objGetObjectResponse.ResponseStream))
            {
//Read response.
                Console.WriteLine("Contents :" +
                objStreamReader.ReadToEnd());
            }
        }
    }
```

How it works...

AD FS integration is an important organization because their users don't need to use a different set of credentials for AWS access. The proxy application used to get temporary credentials from AWS **Security Token Service** (**STS**) should be a domain-joined machine. The proxy server stores the mapping between the user and the policy. To retrieve temporary credentials, the proxy server needs `AccessKeyId` and `SecretAccessKey`. We create an IAM user, assign the permissions, and create access keys for the user.

Before creating the sample application, download the .Net SDK using NuGet packager. In Visual Studio's NuGet console, run the following command. After running the command, add the namespace to your project.

```
Install-Package AWSSDK
```

The machine running the client application should be a domain-joined machine. In the client application, you call proxy service to get the temporary credentials and access the S3 data from user folder.

Configuring AWS multifactor authentication

AWS **multifactor authentication** (**MFA**) adds an extra layer of security for your AWS users. MFA verifies your identity through something you know (user ID and password) and something you have with you (hardware device or software token). In addition to the user name and password, the user will need to enter a one-time authentication code while logging into the AWS console. As a best practice always configure multifactor authentication for the root account and other highly privileged IAM users. MFA is also used to control access to a specific resource and to AWS service API calls.

Using conditions in the policy, you can specifically allow a user access to a set of services only if the user was authenticated using the MFA code. For example, you can specify a condition that a user is allowed to create or terminate EC2 instances in the production environment only if they are authenticated using MFA.

There are two types of MFA—virtual and hardware. The virtual MFA device uses an application to generate an authentication code that is compatible with **time-based one-time password** (**TOPT**) standard. There are several different virtual MFA apps that you can use however note that AWS requires the virtual MFA app to generate a six-digit code. Virtual MFA is free to use, and you will need to either download the official MFA app or use Google Authenticator from your smartphone to implement MFA.

In case you want to implement hardware-based MFA, then you will need to purchase the hardware MFA device from third-party vendors such as Gemalto.

In this recipe, we configure a virtual MFA device (Google Authenticator) with AWS IAM.

How to do it...

1. Create a virtual MFA device.

   Execute the following command to create a virtual MFA device for the `ethanhunt` user. Record the serial number for further use.

   ```
   $ aws iam create-virtual-mfa-device
   --virtual-mfa-device-name ethanhuntmfadevice
   --outfile F:\\ethanhuntmfadevice.txt
   --bootstrap-method Base32StringSeed
   ```

2. Enable the virtual MFA device.

   Execute the following command to enable the MFA device. The user-name parameter specifies `ethanhunt`, the user for whom you want to enable the MFA device.

   ```
   $ aws iam enable-mfa-device
   --user-name ethanhunt
   --serial-number arn:aws:iam::968336292411:mfa/ ethanhuntmfadevice
   --authentication-code-1 244672
   --authentication-code-2 705514
   ```

How it works...

First, we create the virtual MFA device. In the command, we specify the name of the virtual MFA device, output file path where the bootstrap information stored, and the method to be used to seed the virtual MFA, for example, `QRCodePNG` or `Base32StringSeed`. The seed information should be destroyed after the virtual device is provisioned.

After executing the command, the result file contains the configuration key. Manually, enter this configuration key in your Google Authenticator app. Make sure to select the **Time base** checkbox. After entering the configuration key, copy two consecutive codes from Google Authenticator app, which are required to associate virtual MFA device with the specific user.

In the command used to enable the MFA device, we associate the MFA device with the user, specify the IAM user name, the device ARN (MFA serial number), and the authentication code emitted by the device.

There's more...

The virtual MFA app can run on smartphones, which makes them more convenient than hardware MFA devices. However, this also makes virtual MFA less secure than hardware MFA. Save the secret key in a secure place when you configure the virtual MFA device. This will help you reconfigure the app to use the same virtual MFA in case you lose your phone.

As you need to have physical access to the smartphone or hardware device to configure the virtual MFA, it is preferable to grant the users access to provision and manage their MFA devices. In addition, you can deny these users access to AWS resources until they authenticate using their provisioned MFA device.

5

Monitoring Amazon EC2 Instances

In this chapter, we will cover recipes for:

- ▶ Collecting EC2 metrics using AWS CloudWatch
- ▶ Collecting custom metrics from EC2 instances
- ▶ Monitoring costs using CloudWatch
- ▶ Sending an e-mail based on a CloudWatch alarm
- ▶ Using CloudWatch Logs

Introduction

Amazon CloudWatch is AWS's monitoring service. It can be used to monitor your applications and AWS resources. AWS CloudWatch works with all key AWS services including EC2, RDS, DynamoDB, Elastic MapReduce, Kinesis, CloudSearch, and so on. CloudWatch provides several out-of-the-box metrics such as CPU utilization, network utilization, and disk I/O metrics from EC2 instances. However, you can also collect custom metrics from your applications.

AWS Management Console can be used to view, search, and graph the metrics data loaded by Amazon CloudWatch. CloudWatch stores data as a series of time stamped data points.

One of most common use cases for CloudWatch is to use it to set alarms and take actions, based on the metrics. For example, you can stop, terminate, recover, or reboot an EC2 instance in response to a CloudWatch alarm being raised. CloudWatch Logs lets you collect your application, system, and custom log files into AWS CloudWatch Logs for analysis.

AWS CloudWatch dashboard is used to visualize the metrics. You can also build customized dashboards for your CloudWatch metrics. The data for these dashboards can be pulled in from multiple regions to provide an overall view of your environment.

In addition, you can create specific CloudWatch alarms to alert the user via e-mail or autoscale your application tiers based on the metrics. CloudWatch can also be used to manage your costs, for example, deleting idle instances or alerting you when costs exceed a certain threshold.

Collecting EC2 metrics using AWS CloudWatch

You can collect basic metrics such as CPU utilization, network I/O, and disk I/O metrics from your EC2 instances. There are two types of CloudWatch monitoring services—basic and detailed. In **basic monitoring**, the Amazon EC2 metrics data is collected at 5 minute periods and retained for 2 weeks, at no charge. The metrics are preselected and limited in number. Basic monitoring is automatically enabled for all EC2 instances. In **detailed monitoring**, the metrics are collected at 1-minute intervals and charged per hour per instance.

Regardless of the monitoring type, the metrics are aggregated by autoscaling group and EBS (if you are using autoscaling or EBS). If you want detailed monitoring, you can enable it, both while creating a new EC2 instance and for existing EC2 instances. You can access the metrics data using either the CloudWatch API or the AWS Management Console.

How to do it...

1. Enable detail monitoring when launching an instance.

   Execute the following command to create an EC2 instance with detail monitoring enabled. Create VPC, subnet, security group, and key/pair before running the following command:

   ```
   $ aws ec2 run-instances
   --image-id ami-7e2c612c
   --count 1
   --instance-type t1.micro
   --key-name ApacheServerKeyPair
   --security-group-ids sg-f332ea96
   --subnet-id subnet-5314c936
   --monitoring Enabled=value??
   ```

2. List metrics.

    Execute the following command to list the metrics you are collecting for AWS EC2:

    ```
    $ aws cloudwatch list-metrics --namespace AWS/EC2
    ```

3. Get metric statistics.

    Execute the following command to retrieve specific statistics, for example, the average CPU utilization of our EC2 instance (`i-54cfb999`):

    ```
    $ aws cloudwatch get-metric-statistics
    --metric-name CPUUtilization
    --start-time 2015-04-09T15:00:00
    --end-time 2015-04-09T16:00:00
    --period 300
    --namespace AWS/EC2
    --statistics Average
    --dimensions Name=InstanceId,Value=i-54cfb999
    ```

How it works...

In the first step, we enable detail monitoring for our EC2 instance while creating it, by specifying the monitoring parameter. In AWS CloudWatch, namespaces are containers for metrics. All AWS services that provide Amazon CloudWatch data use a namespace string, beginning with `AWS/`. For example, the namespace for EC2 is `AWS/EC2`. Metrics in different namespaces are isolated from each other.

Dimension is a name/value pair that uniquely identifies a metric. AWS services that provide AWS CloudWatch data also attach dimensions to each metric. You can use the dimensions for EC2 instances, for example, `ImageId`, `InstanceId`, `InstanceType`, and so on, to refine or filter the metrics returned.

The `list-metrics` command returns a list of metrics stored for the AWS account. The output of the `list-metrics` command contains a token to paginate through the results. The namespace parameter in the `list-metrics` command helps in filtering the results for EC2 instances.

After listing the metrics, we retrieve statistical data for a given metric (using the `get-metrics-statistics` command) based on the namespace, metric, start and end times, period or granularity of the data points (in seconds), the return values, and the dimensions. In our example, we compute the average CPU utilization for a specific instance.

For a list of namespaces, refer to the following link:
`http://docs.aws.amazon.com/AmazonCloudWatch/`
`latest/DeveloperGuide/aws-namespaces.html`

Collecting custom metrics from EC2 instances

You can collect custom metrics from your applications, for example, the number of active sessions, response latency, and many more. More importantly, you can report custom metrics in application and business terms. For example, average number of orders processed per minute, today, on an e-commerce site. These business metrics can help you with capacity planning and allocating suitable budgets for your cloud infrastructure based on the business impact.

Custom metrics help you monitor your applications, directly, from CloudWatch. Using these custom metrics, you can create alarms that can, for example, add instances in the autoscaling group. There is a simple PUT API call to collect custom metrics. AWS also provides monitoring scripts for Linux and Windows that send custom metrics to the AWS CloudWatch.

How to do it...

1. Installing AWS Java SDK.

    It helps you access AWS CloudWatch service from Java applications. In your Maven dependency section, add the following dependency for AWS Java SDK Version 1.9.28.1:

    ```
    <dependency>
        <groupId>com.amazonaws</groupId>
        <artifactId>aws-java-sdk</artifactId>
        <version>1.9.28.1</version>
    </dependency>
    ```

2. Collecting custom metrics from the EC2 instance.

    In our example program here, we collect custom metrics into AWS CloudWatch. The Java program inserts session metric into AWS CloudWatch:

    ```
    // Insert custom metrics into CloudWatch.
        public static void InsertMetric() {

    // Create BasicAWSCredentials with Access Key Id and Secret
    Access Key.
    ```

```
        BasicAWSCredentials credentials = new
        BasicAWSCredentials(
              "Access Key Id",
              "Secret Access Key");

// Create CloudWatch client.
        AmazonCloudWatchClient cloudWatchClient = new
        AmazonCloudWatchClient(
              credentials);

// Set endpoint.
        cloudWatchClient.setEndpoint("monitoring.ap-
        southeast-1.amazonaws.com");

// Initialize PutMetricDataRequest.
        PutMetricDataRequest putMetricDataRequest = new
        PutMetricDataRequest();

// Set Namespace.
        putMetricDataRequest.setNamespace("Production");

// Initialize Dimension.
        Dimension dimension = new Dimension();

// Set dimension name.
        dimension.setName("ApacheInstance");

// Set dimesion value.
        dimension.setValue("app01");

// Initialize MetricDatum.
        MetricDatum sessionMetric = new MetricDatum();

// Add dimension.
        sessionMetric.getDimensions().add(dimension);

// Set metric name.
        sessionMetric.setMetricName("SessionMetric");

// Set timestamp.
        sessionMetric.setTimestamp
        (Calendar.getInstance().getTime());

// Set value.
        sessionMetric.setValue(1.0);
```

```
// Add metric to request.
        putMetricDataRequest.getMetricData()
        .add(sessionMetric);

// Send metric request to CloudWatch.
        cloudWatchClient.putMetricData
        (putMetricDataRequest);
}
```

3. Get metric statistics.

The following Java program retrieves statistics for the metric we created earlier:

```
// Retrieve statistics for the specified metric.
    public static void GetMetricStatistics() {

// Create BasicAWSCredentials with Access Key Id and Secret
Access Key.
        BasicAWSCredentials credentials = new
        BasicAWSCredentials("Access Key Id",
                            " Secret Access Key ");

// Create CloudWatch client.
        AmazonCloudWatchClient cloudWatchClient = new
        AmazonCloudWatchClient(credentials);

// Set endpoint.
        cloudWatchClient.setEndpoint("monitoring.ap-
        southeast-1.amazonaws.com");

// Initialize GetMetricStatisticsRequest.
        GetMetricStatisticsRequest
        getMetricStatisticsRequest=new
        GetMetricStatisticsRequest();

// Set namespace.
        getMetricStatisticsRequest.setNamespace
        ("Production");

// Initialize Dimension.
        Dimension dimension = new Dimension();

// Set dimension name.
        dimension.setName("ApacheInstance");

// Set dimesion value.
```

```
        dimension.setValue("app01");

// Add dimension to request.
        getMetricStatisticsRequest.getDimensions()
        .add(dimension);

// The metric statistics to return. Valid values are
Average, Sum,
// SampleCount, Maximum and Minimum.
        List<String> statistics = new ArrayList<String>();

// Get average value.
        statistics.add("Average");

// Add to request.
        getMetricStatisticsRequest.setStatistics
        (statistics);

// The granularity, in seconds, of the returned data
points.
        getMetricStatisticsRequest.setPeriod(300);

// Get the calender object.
        Calendar cal = Calendar.getInstance();

// Get the current time.
        Date now = cal.getTime();

// Reset hours.
        cal.add(Calendar.HOUR, -1);

// Get one hour back time.
        Date oneHourBack = cal.getTime();

// The time stamp to use for determining the first data
point to return.
        getMetricStatisticsRequest.setStartTime
        (oneHourBack);

// The time stamp to use for determining the last data
point to return
        getMetricStatisticsRequest.setEndTime(now);

// Set metric name
```

```
        getMetricStatisticsRequest.setMetricName
        ("SessionMetric");

// Get metric statistics.
        GetMetricStatisticsResult result = cloudWatchClient
        .getMetricStatistics(getMetricStatisticsRequest);

// Get the label.
        String lable = result.getLabel();

// Get the data points of specified metric.
        List<Datapoint> datapoints =
        result.getDatapoints();

// Iterate through data points.
        for (Datapoint datapoint : datapoints) {

// The average of metric values that correspond to the
datapoint.
            double avg = datapoint.getAverage();

// The time stamp used for the datapoint.
            Date timeStamp = datapoint.getTimestamp();
        }
    }
```

How it works...

In this recipe, we showed you the steps for collecting custom metrics from a Java program. In the first step, we need to install the AWS Java SDK. In our example, we used Production as our namespace. In order to uniquely identify each Apache server in our production deployment, we added the ApacheInstance dimension with a value of app01. Each Apache server in the production deployment is going to have this value for the dimension. Instead of hardcoding access key ID and secret access key, we can create the EC2 instance with an IAM role that has the access to CloudWatch. Using CloudWatch API, you can create your own dashboards and graphs based on the statistics. In our example, we insert the active user count metric into CloudWatch.

There's more...

We can use Elastic Beanstalk to gather and analyze additional health information on your environment. Elastic Beanstalk uses a health agent to monitor server logs and system metrics along with EBS data ad autoscaling to provide detailed health-related information on the EC2 instances. This information uses colors (green, red, and yellow), an indicator for the severity of the issues and a message indicating the cause. The health status can be viewed in real time on the AWS Management Console or through CLI commands. To record and track the enhanced health reporting over time, the information gathered by Elastic Beanstalk can be published to Amazon CloudWatch.

Monitoring costs using CloudWatch

AWS CloudWatch can help you track and manage your cloud costs. This is especially useful where your AWS resource usage varies significantly and you need to log in to the AWS portal several times a day to track the usage. You can set appropriate alarms when the charges exceed a certain predefined threshold. To enable billing alerts for your AWS account, you have to log in as the account owner and edit the configuration settings. Hence, you can send notifications based on these metrics as e-mails and/or route them to other applications for further processing.

The estimated charges are calculated and sent several times a day to CloudWatch. These metrics include estimated total charges and charges by service. In addition, if you are using the consolidated billing option, then your CloudWatch metrics for estimated charges by linked account and estimated charges by linked account and service are also stored. This data is stored for 2 weeks, and it includes the estimated charges for every AWS service you use, as well as the total costs.

How to do it...

Enabling the monitoring of your estimated charges

You can enable the monitoring of your estimated charges in the AWS portal. To enable detail monitoring follow these steps:

1. Open AWS billing console at `https://console.aws.amazon.com/billing/home#/`.

2. Log in to the AWS console using the username and password.

3. Click on **Preferences**.

4. Select the **Receive Billing Alerts** checkbox:

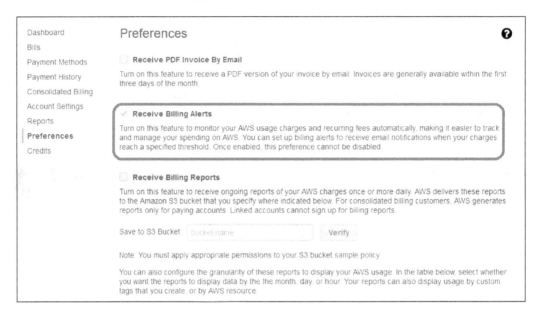

5. Create an SNS topic.

    Execute the following command to create the SNS topic called `BillingTopic`. Record `TopicArn` for further usage.

    ```
    $ aws sns create-topic
    --name BillingTopic
    ```

6. Subscribe to the SNS topic by running the following command. A user with e-mail ID `ethan@awscloud.com` is subscribed to an SNS topic called `BillingTopic`.

    ```
    $ aws sns subscribe
    --topic-arn
    arn:aws:sns:ap-southeast-1:968336292411:BillingTopic
    --protocol email
    --notification-endpoint ethan@awscloud.com
    ```

7. Create the billing alarm.

    Execute the following command to create an alarm that sends e-mail notifications to user when your estimated month-to-date charges for Amazon EC2 exceeds $50.

    ```
    $ aws cloudwatch put-metric-alarm
    --alarm-name ec2billing
    --comparison-operator GreaterThanOrEqualToThreshold
    ```

```
--evaluation-periods 1

--metric-name EstimatedCharges

--namespace AWS/Billing

--dimensions Name=Currency,Value=USD

--period 21600

--statistic Maximum

--threshold 50

--actions-enabled

--alarm-actions arn:aws:sns:ap-southeast-
1:968336292411:BillingTopic
```

How it works...

First, we enable detail monitoring using the AWS console. Next, we create an SNS topic and subscribe to it. After the user subscribes to the topic, he/she will receive a confirmation mail from AWS. After the user confirms the subscription, he/she will start receiving the alerts as e-mail from AWS.

The protocol parameters let us specify the protocol from the supported protocols (HTTP, HTTPS, e-mail, email-JSON, SMS, SQS, etc). You can construct systems that react to the alarms via a HTTP(S) endpoint poke from these alerts. We also specify the endpoint for the notifications. The endpoints vary by the protocol selected. For example, for the in the e-mail protocol, the notification endpoint is the e-mail address.

We create the billing alarm based on the metric data. In our example, we send out an e-mail notification when the charges hit a certain amount. The alarm action here is the SNS topic with name BillingTopic, and the users subscribed to this topic will receive e-mails when the alarm is triggered. We assign a name to the alarm, the arithmetic operation to use when comparing the specified statistic and threshold, the number of periods over which data is compared to the specified threshold, the metric, namespace, period, statistic, and the threshold value.

> If you are new to the AWS environment, then a good starting point is to set up a billing alert for restricting your usage to remain within the free usage tier. Later on, you can set the limit to remain within your assigned or planned budgets.

The actions-enabled parameter also indicates whether or not actions should be executed during any changes to the alarm's state and the AlarmActions parameter lists the actions to execute when this alarm is triggered. Each action is specified as an **Amazon Resource Name (ARN)**.

Sending an e-mail based on a CloudWatch alarm

This recipe is similar to the previous one. However, in this case, we set up metrics, alarms, and notifications that are vital to the operations team. CloudWatch alarms help you notify users by e-mail, if any of the specified metrics cross their predefined thresholds. For example, you can collect latency metrics from the ELB and trigger an alarm that sends an e-mail notification to the operations team, if the latency exceeds 60 milliseconds. CloudWatch uses **Simple Notification Service** (**SNS**) to send these e-mails. The administrators and operations teams subscribe to this SNS topic to receive the CloudWatch notifications.

How to do it...

1. Create an SNS topic.

   In the following example, the command creates the SNS topic called `EC2CpuHighTopic`. Record `TopicArn` for further usage.

   ```
   $ aws sns create-topic
   --name EC2CpuHighTopic
   ```

2. Subscribe to the SNS topic.

   Execute the following command to specify the e-mail ID `ethan@awscloud.com` subscribed to the SNS topic called `EC2CpuHighTopic`.

   ```
   $ aws sns subscribe
   --topic-arn
   arn:aws:sns:ap-southeast-1:968336292411:EC2CpuHighTopic
   --protocol email
   --notification-endpoint ethan@awscloud.com
   ```

3. Send an e-mail notification based on the CloudWatch alarm.

   Execute the following command to create a CloudWatch alarm that sends an e-mail notification to the operations team when the average CPU utilization goes above 70%. Replace `InstanceId` with your instance ID.

   ```
   $ aws cloudwatch put-metric-alarm
   --alarm-name cpuhigh
   --alarm-description "Alarm when CPU exceeds 70 percent"
   --metric-name CPUUtilization
   --namespace AWS/EC2
   --statistic Average
   ```

```
--period 300
--threshold 70
--comparison-operator GreaterThanThreshold
--dimensions  Name=InstanceId,Value=i-54cfb999
--evaluation-periods 2
--alarm-actions
arn:aws:sns:ap-southeast-1:968336292411:EC2CpuHighTopic
```

4. Test CloudWatch alarm.

   Execute the following command to set the alarm state from INSUFFICIENT_DATA to OK. The possible states are OK (the metric is within the defined threshold), ALARM (the metric is outside of the defined threshold), and INSUFFICIENT_DATA (the alarm has just started, the metric is not available, or not enough data is available for the metric to determine the alarm state).

   ```
   $ aws cloudwatch set-alarm-state
   --alarm-name cpuhigh
   --state-reason "Alarm Testing"
   --state-value OK
   ```

5. Execute the following command to change the alarm state from OK to ALARM:

   ```
   $ aws cloudwatch set-alarm-state
   --alarm-name cpuhigh
   --state-reason "Alarm Testing"
   --state-value ALARM
   ```

How it works...

The steps in this recipe are exactly the same as the previous one except that we included a testing step to test the alarm. Note that alarms invoke actions for sustained state changes over a defined number of time periods.

As a best practice, you should always test your alarms and alerts to ensure that they are functioning as expected. You can test your CloudWatch alarms using AWS CLI. We execute commands to temporarily set the state of the alarm for our testing. We specify the alarm name, the reason for setting the alarm to the specific state, and the value of the state. Ensure that you receive the e-mail notification setup for the alarm.

Using CloudWatch Logs

AWS CloudWatch Logs helps you store, monitor, and analyze your application, system and custom logs, centrally. Using CloudWatch Logs you can monitor your logs in near real time for specific errors and exceptions in your application. For example, you might want to monitor exceptions such as `NullPointerException`, `ArrayIndexOutOfBounds`, and `ArithmeticException` in your Java application.

We will need to aggregate the logs from multiple hosts in an environment where instances are added and deleted, dynamically. AWS CloudWatch is not restricted to work with EC2 instances only, it can also be used for on-premise servers and servers hosted on other public clouds. You can analyze your logs and archive them for access later.

You can extract metrics from logs as they come into AWS CloudWatch using the metric filter. For example, you may want to monitor your web server logs for 4xx and 5xx status codes or monitor your server's log files for OS specific error conditions. In addition, you may also create alarms with predefined thresholds, notifications, and actions for these conditions.

How to do it...

1. Create an IAM role for the EC2 instance.

    Create a JSON document with the content specified here, and save it as `CloudWatchRoleForEC2.json`:

    ```
    {
        "Version": "2012-10-17",
        "Statement": {
            "Effect": "Allow",
            "Principal": {"Service": "ec2.amazonaws.com"},
            "Action": "sts:AssumeRole"
        }
    }
    ```

2. Execute the following command to create the `CloudWatchRoleForEC2` using the JSON document:

    ```
    $ aws iam create-role
    --role-name CloudWatchRoleForEC2
    --assume-role-policy-document
    file://F:\\CloudWatchRoleForEC2.json
    ```

3. Assign permissions to the role.

4. Create an inline policy for the role.

   Create a JSON document with the following content. Save the file as `CloudWatchRoleForEC2Policy.json`.

   ```json
   {
       "Version": "2012-10-17",
       "Statement": [
           {
           "Effect": "Allow",
             "Action": [
               "logs:*"
           ],
               "Resource": "arn:aws:logs:*:*:*"
           }
       ]
   }
   ```

5. Execute the following command to assign the inline policy (`CloudWatchRoleForEC2Policy`) to the role:

   ```
   $ aws iam put-role-policy
   --role-name CloudWatchRoleForEC2
   --policy-name CloudWatchRoleForEC2Policy
   --policy-document
   file://F:\\CloudWatchRoleForEC2Policy.json
   ```

6. Create an instance profile.

   Execute the following command to create an instance profile named `CloudWatchRoleForEC2Profile`:

   ```
   $ aws iam create-instance-profile
   --instance-profile-name CloudWatchRoleForEC2Profile
   ```

7. Add role to an instance profile.

   Execute the following command to add a role named `CloudWatchRoleForEC2` to the instance profile named `CloudWatchRoleForEC2Profile`.

   ```
   $ aws iam add-role-to-instance-profile
   --instance-profile-name CloudWatchRoleForEC2Profile
   --role-name CloudWatchRoleForEC2
   ```

8. Launch the EC2 instance with role.

    Execute the following command to create an EC2 instance using the instance profile. However, before executing the command, you must create the key pairs, security groups, VPC, and the subnet.

    ```
    $ aws ec2 run-instances
    --image-id ami-7e2c612c
    --count 1
    --instance-type t1.micro
    --key-name ApacheServerKeyPair
    --security-group-ids sg-f332ea96
    --subnet-id subnet-5314c936
    --iam-instance-profile Name=CloudWatchRoleForEC2Profile
    ```

9. Configure the CloudWatch Log agent to capture specific events from the `/var/log/messages` files.

10. By running the following command, you can download the CloudWatch Log agent.

    Execute the following commands on earlier created EC2 instance:

    ```
    wget
    https://s3.amazonaws.com/aws-cloudwatch/downloads/latest/awslogs-agent-setup.py
    ```

11. Set up the agent.

    Execute the following command to set up the agent:

    ```
    python ./awslogs-agent-setup.py --region ap-southeast-1
    ```

```
Step 3 of 5: Configuring AWS CLI ...
AWS Access Key ID [None]:
AWS Secret Access Key [None]:
Default region name [ap-southeast-1]:
Default output format [None]:

Step 4 of 5: Configuring the CloudWatch Logs Agent ...
Path of log file to upload [/var/log/syslog]: /var/log/messages
Destination Log Group name [/var/log/messages]:

Choose Log Stream name:
  1. Use EC2 instance id.
  2. Use hostname.
  3. Custom.
Enter choice [1]: 1

Choose Log Event timestamp format:
  1. %b %d %H:%M:%S     (Dec 31 23:59:59)
  2. %d/%b/%Y:%H:%M:%S (10/Oct/2000:13:55:36)
  3. %Y-%m-%d %H:%M:%S (2008-09-08 11:52:54)
  4. Custom
Enter choice [1]: 1

Choose initial position of upload:
  1. From start of file.
  2. From end of file.
Enter choice [1]: 1
More log files to configure? [Y]: n

Step 5 of 5: Setting up agent as a daemon ...DONE
```

12. Retrieve logged events.

    Execute the following command to retrieve the logged events from AWS CloudWatch Logs for instance with ID i-07eb9aca in the log group with the name webserver.

    ```
    $ aws logs get-log-events
    --log-group-name webserver
    --log-stream-name i-07eb9aca
    ```

How it works...

We need to install an agent on the Linux or Windows machines to get the logs into AWS CloudWatch Logs. If you have lots of machines to install, then you can use Chef or AWS CloudFormation. We started by creating a role and assigning suitable permissions using a policy. We created a policy for allowing access to AWS CloudWatch Logs from the EC2 instance. If you use the AWS console for creating the role, AWS automatically creates the instance profile with the same name as role. However, as we created the role from the command line, we needed to create the instance profile, and then added the role to the instance profile.

After creating the role, we launched our EC2 instance with the IAM role. We specified the ID of the image, number of instances to create, type of EC2 instance, key/pair name (for authentication), security group IDs, the subnet, and the IAM instance profile name.

Running AWS CloudWatch Logs agent requires AWS access key ID and AWS secret access key. However, we launched the EC2 instance with the IAM role so that we could ignore these two values (by pressing enter). We specified the log stream name, log group name, timestamp, and the AWS region. Here, we logged the `/var/log/messages` file into AWS CloudWatch.

> Log stream is a sequence of log events that share the same source. For example, all log events coming from particular application instance.
>
> A log group is a group of log streams that share the same retention and access controls.

Finally, we retrieved the logged events by specifying the log group and log stream parameters.

There's more...

For capturing security-related events, such as failed login attempts, you can define the metric filter on the `/var/log/security` file. You can set an alarm and send a notification to the appropriate people in case the threshold for too many failed login attempts is exceeded.

If you want to monitor API calls made against your account, then you need to leverage Amazon CloudWatch's integration with AWS CloudTrail, and you can configure CloudTrail to send logs to CloudWatch Logs. This enables you to monitor CloudTrail Log events. Furthermore, you can create alarms, set up SNS notifications, use metric filter, or execute actions against events triggered by a specific API activity (as captured by AWS CloudTrail). For example, you can create such alarms for changes to CloudTrail events such as changes to the security group configuration and/or network ACLs.

You can use AWS CloudFormation templates to create CloudWatch metric filters and alarms. For example, you can download and edit a sample CloudFormation template, containing filters and alarms that enable you to receive notifications when certain CloudTrail events such as security-related API calls are made.

6
Using AWS Data Services

In this chapter, we will cover recipes for:

- ▶ Using Amazon SimpleDB services from a Java program
- ▶ Using Amazon DynamoDB
- ▶ Using Amazon ElastiCache
- ▶ Using Amazon RDS

Introduction

Typical multi-tier cloud applications are built using one or more of the AWS data services. These data services include options for both relational and NoSQL workloads. Running and operating NoSQL and relational database servers on premise not only adds to your operations and administrative burden, but also towards the overall cost. AWS provides these highly available and scalable services out of the box. These services have their own programming SDKs to support several different languages such as C#, Java, and others. AWS data services include SimpleDB and DynamoDB NoSQL workloads and AWS ElastiCache for in-memory caching as a service. For relational database workloads, AWS provides the RDS service that is essentially a relational database service.

This chapter focuses on recipes for using these services from Java.

Using Amazon SimpleDB services from a Java program

Amazon SimpleDB is a highly available and flexible NoSQL data store. Unlike schema-driven relational databases, SimpleDB's flexibility allows you to change your data model on the fly. The infrastructure provisioning, software installation and maintenance, and high availability feature for SimpleDB is managed by AWS; thereby, alleviating the need for typical database administration tasks.

SimpleDB consists of domains where each domain stores a set of records or items. Each of the items has a unique key, and is described by a set of attribute/value pairs. It is not necessary for the items to contain all the attributes. The data in a domain is automatically indexed by each of the attributes, hence enabling access by any one or more attributes. There is no need for a predefined schema and schema changes, in response new attributes are added later on. However, you can run queries on the data stored within a specific domain only. You can also choose between consistent and eventually consistent read requests for additional flexibility in meeting the specific performance versus consistency requirements of your application.

You can store, query, and update data items via API/web service calls. SimpleDB provides SDKs to access the stored data from several programming languages. SimpleDB integrates with other AWS services such as EC2, S3, and IAM to provide you with a complete environment to develop secure web-scale applications.

Typical use cases include storing your application logs, centrally, versus storing them on each of your running servers. This is a significant benefit for monitoring and troubleshooting issues in an autoscaled environment. Another good use case for SimpleDB usage is to store **Simple Storage Service** (**S3**) metadata information. SimpleDB can easily provide storage, indexing, and querying abilities on this metadata. For example, you can store your videos on S3 and the associated metadata, including the pointers to the S3 object locations on SimpleDB.

How to do it...

In this section, we present a recipe to use SimpleDB services from a Java program. Follow the steps listed below:

1. Install AWS Java SDK.

   In your Maven dependency section, add the following dependency for AWS Java SDK Version 1.9.28.1:

   ```
   <dependency>
       <groupId>com.amazonaws</groupId>
       <artifactId>aws-java-sdk</artifactId>
       <version>1.9.28.1</version>
   </dependency>
   ```

2. Initialize SimpleDB client.

The following code initializes and returns a SimpleDB client:

```
// Initialize SimpleDB client.
    public static AmazonSimpleDBClient Initialize() {

// Create BasicAWSCredentials with Access Key Id and
Secret Access Key.
    BasicAWSCredentials credentials = new
    BasicAWSCredentials(
            "Access Key Id",
            "Secret Access Key");

// Create SimpleDB client.
    AmazonSimpleDBClient simpleDBClient = new
    AmazonSimpleDBClient(
            credentials);

// Set endpoint.
    simpleDBClient.setEndpoint("sdb.ap-southeast-
    1.amazonaws.com");

// Return client.
    return simpleDBClient;
    }
```

3. Create a domain.

The following code creates a domain with the name `"user"`:

```
// Create SimpleDB domain.
    public static void CreateDomain() {

// Get SimpleDB client.
    AmazonSimpleDBClient simpleDBClient = Initialize();

// Create domain request.
    CreateDomainRequest request = new
    CreateDomainRequest(
        "user");

// Creates domain.
    simpleDBClient.createDomain(request);
    }
```

4. Insert data into SimpleDB domain.

The following code inserts a single user item with the item name `"Andrew"` in the `"user"` domain:

```
// Insert item.
    public static void InsertItem() {

// Get SimpleDB client.
    AmazonSimpleDBClient simpleDBClient = Initialize();

// Name attribute.
    ReplaceableAttribute nameAttribute = new
    ReplaceableAttribute();
    nameAttribute.setName("Name");
    nameAttribute.setValue("Andrew");

// Age attribute.
    ReplaceableAttribute ageAttribute = new
    ReplaceableAttribute();
    ageAttribute.setName("Age");
    ageAttribute.setValue("28");

// City attribute.
    ReplaceableAttribute cityAttribute = new
    ReplaceableAttribute();
    cityAttribute.setName("City");
    cityAttribute.setValue("San Francisco");

// Create collection for attributes.
    Collection<ReplaceableAttribute> item = new
    ArrayList<>();
    item.add(nameAttribute);
    item.add(ageAttribute);
    item.add(cityAttribute);

// Put request.
    PutAttributesRequest request = new
    PutAttributesRequest();

// Set domain name.
    request.setDomainName("user");

// Set item name.
    request.setItemName("andrew");
```

```
// Set item attributes.
    request.setAttributes(item);

// Insert item into domain.
    simpleDBClient.putAttributes(request);
}
```

5. Retrieve the item from the domain.

    The following code retrieves the item with item name "Andrew":

```
// Retrieve item.
    public static void GetItem() {

// Get SimpleDB client.
    AmazonSimpleDBClient simpleDBClient = Initialize();

// Prepare get request.
    GetAttributesRequest request = new
    GetAttributesRequest();

// Set domain name.
    request.setDomainName("user");

// Set item name.
    request.setItemName("andrew");

// Get item from domain.
    GetAttributesResult result =
    simpleDBClient.getAttributes(request);

// Iterate through all attributes.
    for (Attribute attribute : result.getAttributes())
    {

// Get attribute name.
    String name = attribute.getName();

// Get attribute value.
    String value = attribute.getValue();
    }
}
```

How it works...

In the first step, we downloaded AWS Java SDK. This SDK helps us access AWS services from Java applications. Before interacting with SimpleDB, we need to specify the access key ID and secret access key of our AWS account. Instead of hardcoding AWS credentials in our Java code, we can create an IAM role with SimpleDB access permissions and launch the instance with that role.

Next, we create the SimpleDB client object that is used to interact with SimpleDB service.

 All service calls made using the SimpleDB client are blocking calls, and it will not return until the service call is completed.

SimpleDB domains are like database tables. You must create a domain before inserting data into it. So, in the next step, we created a SimpleDB domain. The createDomain operation creates a new domain. The domain name should be unique among all the domains associated with the access key. The client can create a maximum of up to 100 domains per account. If additional domains are required, then they need to be specifically requested from Amazon.

In SimpleDB, items are like rows in a relational database table. Each item has an item name to uniquely identify the item in a given domain. Each item contains attributes, similar to columns. Each attribute has an attribute name and an attribute value. In the next step, we inserted an item using the putAttributes operation. The client may specify new attributes using a combination of name/value parameters. The attributes are also uniquely identified in an item by their name/value pairs. Note that you cannot have an empty string as an attribute name, and two attribute instances cannot have the same names and values. We create PutAttributesRequest as a container for our request, and then pass it to the putAttributes operation for inserting our item.

Lastly, we retrieved the newly inserted item to verify our insert into SimpleDB.

 As Amazon SimpleDB makes multiple copies of the data and uses an eventual consistency update model, an immediate getAttributes operation following a putAttributes operation may not return the requested data.

We use GetAttributesRequest as a container for our request, and then pass it to the getAttributes operation for retrieving our item.

There's more...

Relational databases are typically normalized to minimize duplication of data. These databases contain tables with primary and foreign keys to represent relationships between various tables in the database. We use joins to combine data from the tables to form the result sets for the queries. However, there is no equivalent join operation available in Amazon SimpleDB. Hence, if you need to access the data from multiple domains, you will typically need to execute multiple queries.

In order to avoid multiple queries, it is common to de-normalize your data to better reflect the nature of your queries. This is often achieved by combining the data from multiple domains into a single domain or duplicating the data across multiple domains to support your queries, efficiently. For example, if you have two separate domains for your employee and employee address, then you would need two separate queries to access a specific employee's name and the associated address information. In such a situation, you may want to combine the items in the two domains into one domain, and then pull the employee name and the associated address with a single query.

Similarly, if we had the employee and role information in two separate domains, then we may want to duplicate the employee data in the role domain and vice versa. This data duplication can help support queries, such as the role of a specific employee and employees in a specific role, more efficiently. You have to understand your data and queries really well in order to finalize the degree of de-normalization required in your design.

Data is stored as character strings in Amazon SimpleDB. This can present some challenges in your queries due to lexicographic comparisons. This is true especially for numeric and date data types. For resolving these issues for numeric values, you will need to pad them appropriately. For negative numbers, you will need to add offsets while storing them and subtract the same offset value during retrieval. To reduce your costs, you should do these operations only for the fields used in query comparisons. For resolving issues related to date comparisons, a good approach is to use the ISO 8601 format dates.

Using Amazon DynamoDB

AWS DynamoDB is a widely used NoSQL data store. Typically, relational databases are not the best option for large-scale, data-centric applications. In addition, operating these database servers at scale is complex and expensive. For such use cases, NoSQL data stores, such as Amazon DynamoDB, are an effective solution. DynamoDB can be used as a key/value store or as a document store. It is common to store data as JSON documents.

DynamoDB stores data in tables, and each table contains items. An item is a group of attributes that is uniquely identifiable among all the other items in the table. An item is similar to rows in a relational database table, and an attribute is a data element similar to fields or columns in a relational database. There is no upper limit to the number of items that can be stored in a DynamoDB table. A primary key uniquely identifies the items in a table, and the key values need to be supplied for CRUD operations on a given table.

DynamoDB's flexible schema means that not all the items necessarily contain all the attributes. Amazon DynamoDB lets you specify your throughput needs in terms of units of read capacity and writes capacity for your table. During the creation of a table, you specify your required read and write capacity needs, and Amazon DynamoDB automatically partitions and reserves the appropriate amount of resources to meet your throughput requirements.

DynamoDB runs on **Solid State Disks** (**SSDs**) to give predictable performance. You can update the throughput capacity using the AWS console or DynamoDB API to match your application traffic. AWS manages the infrastructure provisioning, software installation and maintenance, and high availability for the DynamoDB service.

DynamoDB is integrated with other AWS and non-AWS services. For example, you can monitor it using CloudWatch, use IAM to control access to DynamoDB resources, log API calls using Cloutrail, search content using Elasticsearch, and so on.

How to do it...

1. Installing AWS Java SDK.

    In your Maven dependency section, add the following dependency for AWS Java SDK Version 1.9.28.1:

    ```
    <dependency>
        <groupId>com.amazonaws</groupId>
        <artifactId>aws-java-sdk</artifactId>
        <version>1.9.28.1</version>
    </dependency>
    ```

2. Initialize DynamoDB client.

    The following code initializes and returns a DynamoDB client.

    ```
    // Initialize DynamoDB client.
        public static AmazonDynamoDBClient Initialize() {

    // Create BasicAWSCredentials with Access Key Id and
    Secret Access Key.
        BasicAWSCredentials credentials = new
        BasicAWSCredentials(
            "Access Key Id",
            " Secret Access Key");
    ```

```
// Create DynamoDB client.
   AmazonDynamoDBClient dynamoDBClient = new
   AmazonDynamoDBClient(
      credentials);

// Set endpoint.
   dynamoDBClient.setEndpoint("dynamodb.ap-southeast-
   1.amazonaws.com");

// Return client.
   return dynamoDBClient;
}
```

3. Create the DynamoDB table.

    The following code creates DynamoDB table with the name `"user"` and uses `UserId` as the primary key:

```
// Create table.
   public static void CreateTable() {

// Get DynamoDB client.
   AmazonDynamoDBClient dynamoDBClient = Initialize();

// Create attribute definition collection.
   ArrayList<AttributeDefinition> definitions = new
   ArrayList<AttributeDefinition>();

// Add attribute definition for UserId.
   definitions.add(new
   AttributeDefinition().withAttributeName("UserId")
      .withAttributeType("N"));

// Create key schema element collection.
   ArrayList<KeySchemaElement> schema = new
   ArrayList<KeySchemaElement>();

// Set UserId as primary key and type as HASH.
   schema.add(new
   KeySchemaElement().withAttributeName("UserId")
      .withKeyType(KeyType.HASH));

// Set provisioned throughput.
   ProvisionedThroughput throughput = new
   ProvisionedThroughput()
```

```
                        .withReadCapacityUnits(10L)
                        .withWriteCapacityUnits(10L);

        // Prepare create table request.
           CreateTableRequest request = new
           CreateTableRequest()
               .withTableName("user").withKeySchema(schema)
               .withProvisionedThroughput(throughput);

        // Set attribute definitions.
           request.setAttributeDefinitions(definitions);

        // Creates table.
           dynamoDBClient.createTable(request);
        }
```

4. Create the `User` class.

```
@DynamoDBTable(tableName = "user")
public class User {

    public int UserId;

    public String Name;

    public int Age;

    public String City;

    @DynamoDBHashKey(attributeName = "UserId")
    public int getUserId() {
        return UserId;
    }

    public void setUserId(int userId) {
        UserId = userId;
    }

    public String getName() {
        return Name;
    }

    public void setName(String name) {
        Name = name;
    }
```

```
        public int getAge() {          return Age;
        }

        public void setAge(int age) {
            Age = age;
        }

        public String getCity() {
            return City;
        }

        public void setCity(String city) {
            City = city;
        }

    }
```

5. After creating the `User` class, you can use the following function to save the user object into the DynamoDB user table:

```
// Insert item.
    public static void InsertItem() {

    // Get DynamoDB client.
        AmazonDynamoDBClient dynamoDBClient = Initialize();

    // Create mapper object.
        DynamoDBMapper mapper = new
        DynamoDBMapper(dynamoDBClient);

    // Initialize user object.
        User objUser = new User();

    // Set user id.
        objUser.UserId = 123;

    // Set user name.
        objUser.Name = "Andrew";

    // Set age.
        objUser.Age = 28;

    // Set city.
        objUser.City = "San Francisco";
```

```
// Save user item.
    mapper.save(objUser);
}
```

6. Retrieve item from the table.

    The following code illustrates a query for retrieving a user from user table with the
    UserId value 123:

```
 // Retrieve item.
    public static void GetItem() {

// Get DynamoDB client.
    AmazonDynamoDBClient dynamoDBClient = Initialize();

// Create mapper object.
    DynamoDBMapper mapper = new
    DynamoDBMapper(dynamoDBClient);

// Initialize user object.
    User objUser = new User();

// Set user id.
    objUser.UserId = 123;

// Prepare query.
    DynamoDBQueryExpression<User> query = new
    DynamoDBQueryExpression<User>()
            .withHashKeyValues(objUser);

// Retrieve items from DynamoDB.
    List<User> list = mapper.query(User.class, query);

// Iterate through all items.
    for (User user : list) {

// Get user name.
        String userName = user.getName();

// Get user age.
        int userAge = user.getAge();
    }
```

How it works...

In the first step, we downloaded AWS Java SDK. This SDK helps us access AWS services from Java applications. The AWS Java SDK provides an object persistence model to define the relationships between the database tables and the objects. After the mapping is done, the objects map to items in your table, and you can use the object methods for CRUD operations. In turn, the appropriate low-level APIs are invoked for you. The SDK also provides a set of annotations, for example, to map your class to a database table and the class attributes to the corresponding item attribute.

Before interacting with DynamoDB, we need to specify the access key ID and secret access key. Alternatively, we can create an IAM user and assign DynamoDB permissions to him/her, and then use his/her credentials to access DynamoDB.

Next, we create the DynamoDB client object that is used to interact with DynamoDB service.

Next, we create a DynamoDB table. When creating a DynamoDB table, you have to specify a primary key. This primary key uniquely identifies each row in the table. DynamoDB distributes the data based on the hash key element into multiple partitions. DynamoDB supports two types of primary keys, hash-type primary key and the hash and range type primary key.

You can specify the provisioned throughput capacity for read and write operations when you create or update a table. DynamoDB will reserve the required resources to meet your throughput requirements.

A unit of read capacity represents one strongly consistent read per second (or two eventually consistent reads per second) for items of size up to 4 KB. A unit of write represents one write per second for items of size up to 1 KB. You cannot group multiple items in a single read or write operation even if the items are 4 KB or smaller or 1 KB or smaller, respectively.

Items larger than 4 KB require more than one read operation. For example, the number of read operations required for a 7-KB item is 2, and for a 10-KB item is 3. The AWS console can be used to monitor the provisioned and actual throughput, and the provisioned throughput can be appropriately tuned to avoid throttling.

After creating the DynamoDB table, you can insert items into it. An item represents a database row, and each item can have multiple attributes. An attribute represents the database columns. DynamoDB supports multiple data types, including scalar types (number, string, binary, Boolean, and null), multivalued types (string set, number set, and binary set), and document types (list and map). The primary key must be a string, number, or binary.

We specify the DynamoDB table name and primary key attribute name using DynamoDB annotations. Hence, in our create `User` class, we annotate the class with `@DynamoDBTable(tableName = "user")` and the `getUserId` function with `@DynamoDBHashKey(attributeName = "UserId")`.

Lastly, we test our insert by retrieving items from our DynamoDB table. DynamoDB supports both eventually consistent and strongly consistent read options. In eventual consistency, when you read data immediately following a write operation, the response might not reflect the results of the write. However, note that data consistency across the multiple copies of the data is typically reached within a second. Hence, if the read operation is retried after a short time, the result of the write operation is reflected in the response. In the case of strongly consistent reads, the latest post-write operation data is returned. If you use eventually consistent reads versus strongly consistent reads, then you will get twice as many reads per second.

There's more...

DynamoDB supports two kinds of primary keys, a primary key consisting of a hash attribute and a primary key consisting of hash and range attributes. In the first type, the primary key consists of a single attribute—the hash attribute. In the second type, there are two attributes—the hash attribute and the range attribute.

DynamoDB also supports secondary indexes. If you want to access the data using non-key attributes, then you would create these secondary indexes. However, DynamoDB consumes additional capacity units to update the indexes on write operations. You might need to adjust your provisioned capacity over a period of time as more secondary indexes are added to your tables.

There are two querying operations available—query and scan. You can use the query operation to query a table using the hash attribute and an optional range filter or the secondary index key. The Scan operation reads every item in the table or the secondary index, and is an expensive operation for large tables and secondary indexes.

You can download and run DynamoDB on your computer. This can be a good way to learn to work with DynamoDB as well as use it reduce your cloud development costs.

Using Amazon ElastiCache

Amazon ElastiCache is a managed cache service that improves latency and throughput for read-intensive applications. Amazon ElastiCache provides a caching layer for your applications. Instead of querying the databases each time, you can use a caching layer in front of the database layer to get higher query performance.

Each node runs an instance of either Memcached or Redis. However, each node in the cluster is of the same instance type and runs the same caching engine. You basically launch the cluster, get the node names, and then connect the client to it. No changes are required in your application code to access ElastiCache, and you can use your existing Redis and Memcached libraries to connect to the ElastiCache's Redis or Memcached clusters, respectively.

Amazon is responsible for tasks such as provisioning hardware, installing caching software, patch management, failure detection, and recovery. Supported in-memory caching engines are Memcached and Redis. ElastiCache clusters are only accessible from EC2 instances. The cache cluster and its related EC2 instances must be in the same VPC. If you want to access cache cluster from outside its VPC, then you will need to setup EC2 inside the cache VPC to act as a proxy for the outside world.

How to do it...

1. Before creating the ElasticCache cluster, you need to create cache subnet group. Execute the following command to create a cache subnet group named `appcachesubnetgroup`:

   ```
   $ aws elasticache create-cache-subnet-group
   --cache-subnet-group-name appcachesubnetgroup
   --cache-subnet-group-description "Application Cache Subnet Group"
   --subnet-ids subnet-5314c936 subnet-49ca1b2c subnet-0240b575
   ```

2. Create a Memcached cluster.

   Execute the following command to create an ElastiCache cluster with three nodes. This cluster uses Memcached as the cache engine.

   ```
   $ aws elasticache  create-cache-cluster
   --cache-cluster-id appcachecluster
   --engine memcached
   --cache-node-type cache.t2.small
   --num-cache-nodes 3
   --engine-version 1.4.14
   --cache-subnet-group-name appcachesubnetgroup
   ```

3. Add an ingress rule for the Memcached port.

   Execute the following command to add an ingress rule for the security group `sg-f332ea96`:

   ```
   $ aws ec2 authorize-security-group-ingress
   --group-id sg-f332ea96
   --protocol tcp
   --port 11211
   --cidr 0.0.0.0/0
   ```

4. Get ElastiCache information to verify your cluster.

   ```
   $ aws elasticache describe-cache-clusters
   --cache-cluster-id appcachecluster
   ```

Working with ElasticCache

The following steps illustrate how you can use ElastiCache from your code.

1. Sign in to the AWS console at `https://console.aws.amazon.com/elasticache/`.

2. Click on **ElastiCache Cluster Client**, and then click on **Download**.

3. After downloading client, extract the ZIP file and add the `AmazonElastiCacheClusterClient-1.0.jar` to the Java application build path.

4. The following sample code connects to the ElastiCache cluster and calls the setter and getter methods. You can retrieve the ElastiCache cluster information like cache cluster DNS name using the `describe-cache-clusters` command.

```
// Create memcached client.
        MemcachedClient client = new MemcachedClient(new
        InetSocketAddress(
    "appcachecluster.nzrwy7.cfg.apse1.cache.amazonaws.com",
    11211));

        // Set value for key andrew.
        client.set("andrew", 3600, 43);

        // Get value.
        int value = (int) client.get("andrew");
```

How it works...

If you want to launch the cache cluster inside the VPC, then you have to create a cache subnet group by defining the appropriate subnet IDs. In the first step, we create the cache subnet group by specifying a name for it, a description, and the subnet IDs.

You can create the ElastiCache cluster with the Memcached engine or Redis engine. Next, we execute the command for creating an ElastiCache cluster with the Memcached engine. For this, we supply the cache cluster ID, the cache engine to use, the compute, and memory capacity of the nodes in the cache cluster, the initial number of cache nodes, the version of the cache engine, and the cache subnet group name. Note that you can retrieve the cache engine version information by executing the `describe-cache-engine-versions` command.

As a best practice, you should restrict ElastiCache node access to applications running on EC2 instances within certain subnet and VPC security groups. In the next step, we add an ingress rule for the Memcached port to allow access from EC2 instances to the cache cluster inside your VPC. We have to add the ingress rule for the cache cluster VPC's default security group. The ingress rule is added by specifying the security group ID, the protocol, the range of ports allowed, and the CIDR IP range. After creating the ElastiCache cluster, we check the details of it by retrieving the cluster information.

Finally, we present some code to illustrate how you can use ElastiCache. You can use your Memcached libraries to access the Memcached engine in the ElastiCache cluster. If you have multiple cache nodes in your cluster, then you have to define all these endpoints in your client code. However, if you use ElastiCache Auto Discovery library, then you don't need to specify the endpoints for all these nodes. In this situation, you have to connect to the configuration endpoint, and then the Auto Discovery library connects to all the other nodes in the cache cluster.

There's more...

You can cache just about anything, including database records, full HTML pages, page fragments, and remote API calls. There are several factors that impact what you should cache. For example, join-based queries, and relatively static but frequently accessed data, are typically good candidates for caching.

Depending on the caching engine, the clustering configurations can vary; for example, Memcached clusters can partition or shard your data across the nodes, whereas Redis supports single node clusters and replication groups, and you cannot partition your data across multiple Redis clusters. In Redis, scaling is achieved by choosing a different node instance type. However, if your application is read-intensive, then you can create multiple read replicas to distribute the load.

Typically, due to its support for sharding, Memcached clusters will tend to use more and smaller nodes while Redis deployments will use fewer, large node instance types. The total memory capacity of your cluster is the product of the number of cache nodes in the cluster and the RAM capacity of each node. You can reduce the impact of a failed node by spreading your caching capacity over a larger number of cache nodes, each with smaller capacity, rather than using a fewer number of high capacity nodes.

You can use the `describe-cache-clusters` command to list the endpoints for a cluster. This command will return the configuration endpoint for a Memcached cluster and the cluster endpoint for a Redis cluster. Additionally, if you specify the `show-cache-node-info` parameter, then this command will also return the endpoints of the individual nodes in the cluster.

A replication group is a collection of Redis clusters, with one primary read-write cluster and several read-only clusters called read replicas. The read replicas are updated asynchronously to remain in sync with the primary cluster. For endpoints in a replication group, you can use the `describe-replication-groups` command. This command returns the replication group's primary endpoint and a list of all the clusters in the replication group with their endpoints.

With Auto-Discovery, your application does not need to manually connect to individual nodes, instead, your application connects to a configuration endpoint. There is no need to hard code individual cache node endpoints in your application because the configuration endpoint DNS entry contains CNAME entries for each of the cache node endpoints. Node Auto-Discovery for Memcached enables automatic discovery of cache nodes by the clients when nodes are added or removed from the cluster. Setup an Amazon SNS topic for ElastiCache, and have an app listen for the add and remove cache node events.

Connecting to a Memcached cluster is done using the cluster's configuration endpoint, while connecting to a Redis cluster is done using its endpoint. Connecting to Redis clusters in a replication group is done using the primary endpoint for all write operations and the individual cluster endpoints for read operations.

 Reference to the ElastiCache user guide is available at `https://aws.amazon.com/documentation/elasticache/` for best practices for using Memcached and Redis clusters in an AWS environment.

Higher availability can be configured through replication across multiple availability zones.

ElastiCache monitors the health of the nodes in a Multi-AZ Replication Group. In case of a failure of the primary node, ElastiCache selects a Read Replica and upgrades it to a primary node. This process can take several minutes and the application design should take this into consideration and continue to operate in the absence of a cache.

Lazy loading is a caching strategy that loads data into the cache only when necessary. Most data is never accessed and only requested data is cached. Cache nodes fail, but the application continues to function, though with increased latency and scale, But a cache miss results in noticeable delay, and the cache data can go stale as it is only updated on a cache miss. However, this can be handled by updating the data in cache whenever the database is updated.

Lazy loading ensures cache is always current. But missing data on scale up can create an issue because the missing data is missing until it is added or updated on the database. Implementing lazy loading in conjunction with a write through strategy can minimize this effect. There can be a lot of data in the cluster that is never read—adding a TTL can help minimize the wasted space.

Using Amazon RDS

Amazon **Relational Database Service** (**RDS**) is a scalable relational database service in the cloud. Supported database engines are MySQL, PostgreSQL, Oracle, Microsoft SQL Server, and MySQL compatible Amazon Aurora engine. No changes are required in your application code to connect to RDS, that is, the code you are already using to connect to databases can be used with Amazon RDS.

Amazon manages the infrastructure provisioning, installing, and maintaining the database software. Database instances using Amazon RDS's MySQL, Oracle, SQL Server, and Oracle engines can be provisioned with General Purpose (SSD) storage, Provisioned IOPS (SSD) storage, or Magnetic storage. If your application needs predictable and consistent I/O performance, you can choose Provisioned IOPS (SSD) instead of using General Purpose (SSD) or Magnetic storage.

You can access RDS via the AWS Management Console, CLI, or API calls. RDS allows to you to efficiently scale compute and storage capacities. In addition, you can launch Read Replicas to offload read-based traffic from your primary database. High-availability features such as Multi-AZ can be configured to synchronously replicate the data to another instance in a different availability zone. In addition, support for automated backups and database snapshots can aid the DR process. SSD-backed storage option provides higher performance for frequently accessed or updated data. You can secure your data by isolating your instances in the VPC, and encrypt your data at rest.

How to do it...

1. Create an RDS DB instance.

   Execute the following command to create an RDS DB instance named appdb and size 30 Gb.

   ```
   $ aws rds create-db-instance
   --db-instance-identifier appdb
   --allocated-storage 30
   --db-instance-class db.m1.small
   --engine mysql
   --master-username admin
   --master-user-password Passw0rd123$
   ```

2. Retrieve DB instance information.

   Execute the following command to retrieve information about DB instance with name appdb in order to verify the details of the RDS instance created:

   ```
   $ aws rds describe-db-instances
   --db-instance-identifier appdb
   ```

3. Download the database driver.

   Add the Maven dependency for the MySQL connector to access the database from the Java code.

```
<dependency>
        <groupId>mysql</groupId>
        <artifactId>mysql-connector-java</artifactId>
        <version>5.1.35</version>
</dependency>
```

4. Create an application database.

   The following sample code illustrates how to create our sample application database, called websupport database, on the RDS instance. Replace RDS DB endpoint, user name, and password with your own specific details.

```
// Create database.
public static void CreateDatabase() throws Exception {

// Register database driver.
        Class.forName("com.mysql.jdbc.Driver");

// Database credentials.
        String userName = "username";
        String password = "password";

// RDS url.
        String dbUrl = "jdbc:mysql://RDS db endpoint/";

// Create connection to RDS instance.
        Connection con = DriverManager.getConnection(dbUrl,
        userName, password);

// Creates a Statement object for sending SQL statements to
the
// database.
        Statement stm = con.createStatement();

// Create database query.
        String sql = "CREATE DATABASE websupport;";

// Execute query.
        stm.executeUpdate(sql);
    }
```

5. Create a table.

   The following code sample creates a table in the application database. Replace the RDS DB endpoint, user name, password, and database name with your own specific details.

   ```
   // Create table.
   public static void CreateTable() throws Exception {

   // Register database driver.
       Class.forName("com.mysql.jdbc.Driver");

   // Database credentials.
       String userName = "username";
       String password = "password";

   // RDS url.
       String dbUrl = "jdbc:mysql://RDS db
       endpoint/websupport";

   // Create connection to RDS instance.
       Connection con = DriverManager.getConnection(dbUrl,
       userName, password);

   // Creates a Statement object for sending SQL
   statements to the
   // database.
       Statement stm = con.createStatement();

   // Create database query.
       String sql = "CREATE TABLE tickets (ID int, frm
       VARCHAR(20),msg VARCHAR(2000));";

   // Execute query.
       stm.executeUpdate(sql);
   }
   ```

6. Insert rows into the table.

   The following sample code inserts a ticket record into the tickets table. Replace RDS DB endpoint, user name, password, and database name with your own specific details.

   ```
   // Insert record.
       public static void InsertRecord() throws Exception {

       // Register database driver.
   ```

```
        Class.forName("com.mysql.jdbc.Driver");

    // Database credentials.
        String userName = "username";
        String password = "password";

    // RDS url.
        String dbUrl = "jdbc:mysql://RDS db
        endpoint/websupport";

    // Create connection to RDS instance.
        Connection con = DriverManager.getConnection(dbUrl,
        userName, password);

    // Creates a Statement object for sending SQL
    statements to the
    // database.
        Statement stm = con.createStatement();

    // Create database query.
        String sql = "INSERT INTO tickets(ID, frm, msg)
        VALUES(1, 'andrew@gmail.com', 'Issue while logging
        into site...');";

    // Execute query.
        stm.executeUpdate(sql);
    }
```

How it works...

In the first step, we created an RDS DB instance with a MySQL database engine. The main parameters, we specify, include a name for the instance, the amount of storage to be initially allocated, compute and memory capacity, the database engine to use, and the user name and password for the master user. After creating the DB instance, you can use the endpoint URL to access the database. Next, we retrieve the information about the newly created DB instance to verify the details (including the endpoint address).

In the next step, we downloaded the database driver, to access the application database from our Java code, by adding a Maven dependency for the MySQL connector. You can use the Connection and Statement classes to access database from your Java programs. The next several steps list the sample code to create an application database, a table, and finally insert a record.

7
Accessing Other AWS Services

In this chapter, we will cover recipes for:

▶ Configuring Route 53

▶ Accessing AWS S3 from applications

▶ Accessing AWS SES from applications

▶ Accessing AWS SNS from applications

▶ Accessing AWS SQS from applications

Introduction

In this chapter, we will cover other services from AWS that help you store files and messages and send e-mails and notifications.

AWS Route 53 provides domain name registration service, DNS, and a health-checking service for your application. You can use any combination of these services. For example, you can use Route 53 as the DNS service to convert domain names to IP addresses for your registered domain name.

AWS **Simple Storage Service** (**S3**) provides a highly scalable and reliable data storage service. You can use S3 to store and retrieve any amount of data, including images, videos, and other content. You can also host and serve your static website from AWS S3.

AWS **Simple Email Service** (**SES**) is an e-mail platform that allows you to send and receive e-mail using your own e-mail address. You add e-mail functionality to any of your applications running on Amazon EC2 via AWS SDKs or the SES API. AWS manages the IP address reputation and the e-mail server and network infrastructure.

AWS **Simple Notification Service** (**SNS**) manages sending messages to the consumers, or subscribers, of the messages. The producers or publishers of messages publish messages to a topic, and the consumers subscribe to the same topic in order to consume the messages. Typical consumers include e-mail addresses, Amazon SQS queues, web servers, and many more. For example, you can use SNS to build push notification functionality for your mobile applications.

Building loosely coupled applications require a queuing service and AWS SQS. A highly available and scalable distributed queuing service is an excellent choice for that.

Configuring Route 53

AWS Route 53 provides domain name registration service, DNS, and a health-checking service for your application. There are SDKs available for many popular programming languages, including Java, Python, NodeJS, Go, .Net, and PHP. If you have a VPC, you can make use of a Private Hosted Zone for Amazon VPC. Using this private DNS, your resources are not accessible outside the VPC. Route 53 supports latency-based routing, if your application is hosted on two different AWS data centers, when the user makes a request, Amazon Route 53 chooses to respond to the DNS query based on which data center gives your user the lowest latency.

How to do it...

1. Installing AWS Java SDK.

    In your Maven dependency section, add the following dependency for AWS Java SDK Version 1.9.28.1. You can find the latest Java SDK version in this link http://mvnrepository.com/artifact/com.amazonaws/aws-java-sdk.

    ```
    <dependency>
        <groupId>com.amazonaws</groupId>
        <artifactId>aws-java-sdk</artifactId>
        <version>1.9.28.1</version>
    </dependency>
    ```

2. Create a hosted zone.

    The following sample program creates a public hosted zone for the cloudinternals. in domain. Before creating the hosted zone, you have to register this domain with the registrar. You can use a registrar such as GoDaddy or AWS Route 53 to register this domain. Record the hosted zone ID for further usage.

    ```
    // Create Hosted Zone.
        public static void CreateHostedZone() {
    ```

```
// Create BasicAWSCredentials with Access Key Id and
Secret Access Key.
    BasicAWSCredentials credentials = new
    BasicAWSCredentials(
            "Access Key Id",
            "Secret Access Key");

// Create Route53 client.
    AmazonRoute53Client route53Client = new
    AmazonRoute53Client(credentials);

// Set endpoint.
    route53Client.setEndpoint("route53.amazonaws.com");

// Prepare hosted zone request.
    CreateHostedZoneRequest request = new
    CreateHostedZoneRequest();

    // Set hosted zone name.
    request.setName("cloudinternals.in");

    // Configuration for hosted zone.
    HostedZoneConfig config = new HostedZoneConfig();

    // Set comment for hosted zone.
    config.setComment("Cloud Internals hosted zone");

    // Set hosted zone configuration.
    request.setHostedZoneConfig(config);

    // Caller reference.
    String callerReference = new Date().toString();

    // Set caller reference.
    request.setCallerReference(callerReference);

    // Create hosted zone.
    CreateHostedZoneResult result =
    route53Client.createHostedZone(request);

    // Get the hosted zone id.
    String hostedZoneId =
    result.getHostedZone().getId();

    // Get delegation set.
```

```
        DelegationSet delegationSet =
        result.getDelegationSet();

        // Get name servers information.
        List<String> nameservers =
        delegationSet.getNameServers();
    }
```

3. Update the registrar's NS records.

   For example, we update our domain's name server records on the GoDaddy website as follows:

   1. Log in to GoDaddy website using link `https://in.godaddy.com/`.
   2. Click on **Domains**.
   3. Click on **Manage My Domains**.
   4. In domain list, select the domain you want to add name server records to.
   5. Click on the **Settings** section.
   6. Click on the **Manage hyperlink** button under the **Nameservers** section.
   7. Select the **Custom** checkbox.
   8. Click on **ADD NAMESERVER** to add name server records.
   9. Add name server records one-by-one and click on **OK**. You can find name server records in the `delegationSet.getNameServers()` response.
   10. Click on **SAVE** to save the changes.

4. Add a recordset to the hosted zone.

   The following sample program adds a record in your hosted zone. This program creates a mapping between a domain named `api.cloudinternals.in` and an IP address `52.74.74.131`.

```
// Create record set.
    public static void CreateRecordSet() {

// Create BasicAWSCredentials with Access Key Id and
Secret Access Key.
    BasicAWSCredentials credentials = new
    BasicAWSCredentials(
            "Access Key Id",
            "Secret Access Key");

// Create Route53 client.
    AmazonRoute53Client route53Client = new
    AmazonRoute53Client(credentials);
```

```
// Set endpoint.
    route53Client.setEndpoint("route53.amazonaws.com");

// Collection of resource records.
    Collection<ResourceRecord> resourceRecords = new
    ArrayList<ResourceRecord>();

// Create resource record.
    ResourceRecord resourceRecord = new
    ResourceRecord();

// Set IP address.
    resourceRecord.setValue("52.74.74.131");

// Add resource record to the list.
    resourceRecords.add(resourceRecord);

// Create resource record set.
    ResourceRecordSet resourceRecordSet = new
    ResourceRecordSet();

// Set domain name for the record set.
    resourceRecordSet.setName("api.cloudinternals.in");

// Set record type.
    resourceRecordSet.setType(RRType.A);

// Resource record cache time to live in seconds.
    resourceRecordSet.setTTL((long) 300);

// Set resource records list.
    resourceRecordSet.setResourceRecords
    (resourceRecords);

// Create change object.
    Change change = new Change();

// Set action to create.
    change.setAction(ChangeAction.CREATE);

// Set resource record set.
    change.setResourceRecordSet(resourceRecordSet);

// Collection of changes.
```

```
            Collection<Change> changes = new
            ArrayList<Change>();

    // Add the change.
        changes.add(change);

    // Create change batch object.
        ChangeBatch changeBatch = new ChangeBatch();

    // Set changes list.
        changeBatch.setChanges(changes);

    // Prepare resource record set request.
        ChangeResourceRecordSetsRequest request = new
        ChangeResourceRecordSetsRequest();

    // Set change batch.
        request.setChangeBatch(changeBatch);

    // Set hosted zone id.
        request.setHostedZoneId("Z2RBSZ6TBBCOGZ");

    // Create A record.
        route53Client.changeResourceRecordSets(request);
    }
```

How it works...

First, we install the AWS SDK, as the AWS Java SDK is required to access the AWS services from Java applications.

A hosted zone contains collection of recordsets, such as a traditional DNS zone file. Each hosted zone contains mapping between domain names and IP addresses. You can manage all your recordsets for a domain in a single hosted zone. After creating the hosted zone, you receive the name server records. Next, we update our register's NS records to route queries for our domain to the Route 53 name servers.

For the hosted zones, resource recordsets, health checks, and cost allocation tags, you have to use the endpoint route53.amazonaws.com. The resource recordsets in a hosted zone must have the same suffix. Domain names, including domains, hosted zones, and resource recordsets consists of labels separated by dots where each label can be up to 63 bytes long and the total length of the domain name is up to 255 bytes.

Finally, we add the recordset to the hosted zone. Creating resource recordsets and choosing a routing policy tells the DNS how you want route the traffic for that domain. For example, you could route the traffic for domain to an on-premise server. There are various types of routing policies available to be used with Route 53, including latency routing policy (based on minimum latency) and geolocation routing policy (based on the location of your users).

There's more...

You can register your domain name with Amazon Route 53 or transfer the registration of existing domains from other registrars to Amazon Route 53. You can use the Route 53 console, Route 53 API, or the AWS SDK for registering and managing your domains. The Route 53 registered domains are configured to renew, automatically. When you register your domain with Amazon Route 53, it is automatically configured as the DNS service for the domain.

Refer to Amazon Route 53 Developer Guide for lists of top-level domains and domain extensions by geography that you can register with Amazon Route 53.

You can use Amazon Route 53 to route queries to AWS resources such as the ELB (public-hosted zones only), Amazon EC2 instances, website hosted in an Amazon S3 bucket (public-hosted zones only), Amazon RDS, and more.

You can configure Route 53 to send automated requests to monitor the health of your web servers. In addition, you can configure CloudWatch alarms for these health checks to send notifications and route traffic to an alternate web server in case one of your web servers becomes unavailable.

Route 53 integrates with IAM, so you control the users who can create a new hosted zone and change resource recordsets. Route 53 is integrated with CloudTrail, so the API calls to Route 53 can be tracked via the CloudTrail Logs.

Accessing AWS S3 from applications

AWS S3 is highly scalable and durable object storage. You only have to pay for the storage you actually use. S3 replicates data in multiple data centers within the region. Further, AWS S3 introduces cross-region replication that replicates your data across AWS regions. In this recipe, we cover both uploading objects to and downloading objects from AWS S3.

How to do it...

1. Installing AWS Java SDK.

   In your Maven dependency section, add the following dependency for AWS Java SDK Version 1.9.28.1:

```
<dependency>
    <groupId>com.amazonaws</groupId>
    <artifactId>aws-java-sdk</artifactId>
    <version>1.9.28.1</version>
</dependency>
```

2. Create a bucket.

The following sample Java program creates a S3 bucket called `laurenceluckinbill` in the Singapore region:

```
// Create S3 bucket.
    public static void CreateBucket() {

        // Create BasicAWSCredentials with Access Key Id
        and Secret Access Key.
        BasicAWSCredentials credentials = new
        BasicAWSCredentials(
                "Access Key Id",
                "Secret Access Key");

        // Create S3 client.
        AmazonS3Client s3Client = new
        AmazonS3Client(credentials);

        // Set endpoint.
        s3Client.setEndpoint("s3-ap-southeast-
        1.amazonaws.com");

        // Create bucket.
        s3Client.createBucket("laurenceluckinbill");

    }
```

3. Upload an object into the S3 bucket. The following sample Java program uploads the `Readme.txt` file into the bucket called `laurenceluckinbill`:

```
// Upload object.
    public static void UploadObject() {

        // Create BasicAWSCredentials with Access Key Id
        and Secret Access Key.
        BasicAWSCredentials credentials = new
        BasicAWSCredentials(
                "Access Key Id",
                "Secret Access Key");
```

```
// Create S3 client.
AmazonS3Client s3Client = new
AmazonS3Client(credentials);

// File to upload.
File file = new File("D:\\Readme.txt");

// Upload object into bucket.
s3Client.putObject("laurenceluckinbill",
"Readme.txt", file);
}
```

4. Download an object.

    The following sample program downloads the Readme.txt object from a bucket called laurenceluckinbill into a local folder:

```
// Download object.
    public static void DownloadObject() {

    // Create BasicAWSCredentials with Access Key Id
    and Secret Access Key.
    BasicAWSCredentials credentials = new
    BasicAWSCredentials(
            "Access Key Id",
            "Secret Access Key");

    // Create S3 client.
    AmazonS3Client s3Client = new
    AmazonS3Client(credentials);

    // Local file path.
    String path = "D:\\Readme.txt";

    // Download object.
    s3Client.getObject(new
    GetObjectRequest("laurenceluckinbill",
            "Readme.txt"), new File(path));
    }
```

How it works...

Objects are stored in containers called buckets on S3. In our example, the object is a file called `Readme.txt` and is stored in a bucket called `laurenceluckinbill`. This object can be accessed using `http://laurenceluckinbill.s3.amazonaws.com/Readme.txt`. S3 provides, both, a REST and a SOAP interface to store and retrieve objects. In addition, AWS SDKs are also provided for building applications that use Amazon S3.

You can configure buckets to be created in a specific region to minimize costs or latency, or meet regulatory requirements. While a bucket is the container on S3, an object is the entity stored in Amazon S3. The objects are uniquely addressed by a combination of the endpoint, bucket, key, and version ID.

First, we install the AWS SDK, as the AWS Java SDK is required to access the AWS services from Java applications.

Next, we create an S3 bucket. We have to create buckets in one of the AWS regions before uploading any data into Amazon S3. We can upload any number of objects inside a bucket. As a best practice, always use DNS-compliant bucket names as it provides support for virtual-host style access to the buckets.

After creating the bucket, you can upload your objects into the bucket or access/download objects from the bucket. In order to upload an object to our bucket, we create an instance of `AmazonS3Client`, and then execute the `putObject` method. The `putObject` method is overloaded. You need to select the appropriate version, depending on whether you are uploading data from a file or a stream. In our example, we are uploading a file from our local drive to our bucket.

The `GetObjectRequest` object provides several options. In our example, we use it to retrieve the object and write to a `File` object on our local drive. Alternatively, the data can be streamed directly from S3, and you can read from it. However, this should be done as quickly as possible because the network connection remains open till you finish reading and close the input stream.

There's more...

Amazon S3 replicates your data across multiple servers, hence your object writes, replacements, and deletes may not be reflected immediately. S3 does not support object locking and the latest request wins. If such a behavior is unacceptable for your application, then you will need to build this functionality. You can also replicate objects to different AWS regions. You can filter by key prefixes to replicate specific objects to specific regions for regulatory or reducing latency.

Each object in Amazon S3 has a storage class associated with it. There are two storage types most commonly used—standard and reduced redundancy storage. You can reduce your costs using the S3 Reduced Redundancy Storage option for storing non-critical data. This option replicates the data fewer number of times than the standard S3 storage, and hence the associated costs are lower as well.

You can enable versioning on your buckets. If enabled, Amazon S3 assigns a unique version ID to your objects. This helps protect you from unintended overwrites and deletes, and retrieving prior versions of your objects. You can also retrieve specific versions of your objects.

For uploading large objects, you can use the multipart upload API. After all the parts are uploaded, Amazon S3 constructs the object and makes it available for you. When you request a multipart upload, S3 returns you an upload ID. You need to use this ID and a part number (to identify the part and its position in the object being uploaded). You can also retrieve the entire object or retrieve it in parts.

You can list your object keys by prefix. Hence, if you choose a common prefix for the names of your related keys, then you can use the list operation to select or browse the keys in a hierarchical manner using the bucket name and the prefix (similar to your local filesystem).

For deleting objects from Amazon S3, you can use the delete API or the Multi-Object delete API depending on whether you are deleting a single or multiple objects, respectively. You need to create an instance of `AmazonS3Client`, and then execute the `deleteObject` method. If versioning is not enabled, then the object is deleted otherwise the operation puts a delete marker on the version and the object disappears from the bucket. Note that if you specify the version in the delete request, the version ID maps to a delete marker for that object. Then, S3 deletes the marker and the object reappears in your bucket.

You can create policies to control access to the buckets and objects. The policies govern the creation, deletion, and listing the contents of buckets. Every request to S3 can be authenticated or anonymous. You can use IAM user access keys or temporary security credentials to access the services. There are two options for protecting your data at rest on S3—server-side encryption and client-side encryption. In server-side encryption you can let Amazon S3 to encrypt and decrypt your data. If you use Client-Side encryption then you encrypt the data in the client and upload it for storage on S3.

You can host static websites in S3 by configuring your bucket for website hosting. This can be done via the AWS Management Console or using the AWS SDKs. All requests to your registered domain are routed to the appropriate S3 website endpoint. You will also need to create appropriate policies to make your S3 content accessible to the public.

You can configure Amazon S3 notifications for certain S3 events such as object creation, object removal, delete marker created for a versioned object, and so on. These events can be published to an SNS topic, SQS queue, or AWS Lambda function. You can also configure notifications to be filtered by the key prefix.

In addition, Amazon S3 is integrated with CloudWatch, so you can collect and analyze metrics for your S3 buckets. You can also create alarms and send notifications if the threshold is exceeded for a specific S3 metric. API calls to S3 can be tracked via CloudTrail Logs.

Accessing AWS SES from applications

Sending e-mails to users from your applications is a very common requirement. Provisioning hardware and installing the mail server software in your own data center adds to the upfront costs, aside from the security and high-availability concerns. AWS **Simple Email Service** (**SES**) is an e-mail platform from AWS. For example, when you want to send e-mail messages, Amazon SES is your outbound e-mail server. Alternatively, you can configure your existing e-mail server to send the e-mails via Amazon SES.

You can track deliveries, bounced messages, complaints, and rejects from the AWS console, or access the same via the SES API. You can view the e-mail volume limits for your account. You can request an increase in your quota by providing some basic information on e-mail content, and many more to AWS. You can use any standard SMTP library or the AWS SDK to interact with SES.

How to do it...

1. Verify the e-mail address.

   Execute the following sample command to verify the e-mail address, for example, `ethan@gmail.com`:

   ```
   $ aws ses verify-email-identity
   --email-address ethan@gmail.com
   ```

2. Installing AWS Java SDK.

   In your Maven dependency section, add the following dependency for AWS Java SDK Version 1.9.28.1:

   ```
   <dependency>
       <groupId>com.amazonaws</groupId>
       <artifactId>aws-java-sdk</artifactId>
       <version>1.9.28.1</version>
   </dependency>
   ```

3. Send an e-mail using the AWS SES SDK.

   Execute the sample program to send an e-mail. The program uses the N. Virginia region for this purpose.

   ```
   // Send Email.
       public static void SendEmail() {
   ```

```java
// List of to addresses.
    String[] TO = new String[] { "ethan@awscloud.com" };

// Email from address.
    String FROM = "ethan@gmail.com";

// Email subject.
    String MAILSUBJECT = "Test Email";

// Email body.
    String BODY = "This is test email.";

// Set to addresses.
    Destination destination = new
    Destination().withToAddresses(TO);

// Create email subject.
    Content subject = new
    Content().withData(MAILSUBJECT);

// Create email body.
    Content textBody = new Content().withData(BODY);
    Body body = new Body().withText(textBody);

// Create a message with the specified subject and
body.
    Message message = new
    Message().withSubject(subject).withBody(body);

// Assemble the email.
    SendEmailRequest request = new
    SendEmailRequest().withSource(FROM)
    .withDestination(destination).withMessage(message);

// Create BasicAWSCredentials with Access Key Id and
Secret Access Key.
    BasicAWSCredentials credentials = new
    BasicAWSCredentials(
       "Access Key Id",
       "Secret Access Key");

// Create SES client.
    AmazonSimpleEmailServiceClient sesClient = new
    AmazonSimpleEmailServiceClient(
    credentials);
```

```
        // Set endpoint.
          sesClient.setEndpoint("email.us-east-
          1.amazonaws.com");

        // Send the email.
          sesClient.sendEmail(request);
        }
```

How it works...

In the first step, we verify our e-mail address. You have to verify the sender e-mail address before sending e-mails from that address in order to prove that you own it. If you have a list of e-mail addresses, then you can also verify your entire domain with SES.

We will receive a verification e-mail from AWS SES service, and after we click on the verification link, the process is completed. You can track the verification status using the AWS console.

Next, we install the AWS SDK, as the AWS Java SDK is required to access the Amazon SES API from our Java application.

You can use any SMTP libraries or AWS SDK to interact with AWS SES service. In our sample program, we use the AWS SDK to send an e-mail. At this time, AWS SES is available in N. Virginia, Oregon, and Ireland regions only. It is recommended to use the nearest AWS region to reduce network latency.

There's more...

You can send an e-mail using Amazon SES using the SES console, SES SMTP interface, or SES API. Typically, the SMTP and SES APIs are used to send bulk e-mails. You can also use the SMTP interface to integrate your existing e-mail server with SES. As a best practice, choose an SES endpoint in a region that is closest to your application.

When you send a message, Amazon SES constructs an e-mail message that consists of a header, a body, and an envelope that is as per the Internet Message Format specification (RFC 5322).

The Amazon SES account can regulate the number and rate at which you can send e-mails. This can protect from getting classified as a spammer and have your e-mails blocked by an ISP. The sending quota defines the maximum number of e-mails you can send in a given 24-hour period. Over time, both your sending limit and the rate are increased. If you try to send an e-mail after you have hit the sending limits, you will encounter a throttling error and your e-mail will be dropped.

Excessive bounce rates and complaints by the e-mail recipients can lead to a reduction or termination of your SES account.

As a best practice, you should test out your e-mail functionality. Use the mailbox simulator provided by Amazon SES. The simulator is basically a set of test e-mail addresses that are used for testing your sending scenarios without impacting sending quota.

 Refer to the Amazon SES Developer Guide for best practices for sending e-mail using Amazon SES.

You can also use Amazon SES to receive e-mails. For receiving e-mails, handle all the underlying operations including communicating with other mail servers, scanning for spam, scanning for viruses, and rejecting e-mails from untrusted sources. It can also route the received e-mails to S3 buckets.

You can create IAM policies to specify the users permitted to perform SES actions.

Accessing AWS SNS from applications

AWS SNS helps you send e-mail, SMS, and mobile push notifications very efficiently. The subscribers of the messages receive the messages over one of the supported protocols such as HTTP/S, SMS, e-mail, and Amazon SQS.

If you are targeting an HTTP(S) endpoint from SNS, then it is highly recommended that your HTTP(S) application be highly available to avoid message drops. For reliable messaging, you can store the notification messages to Amazon SQS.

Mobile push notifications are typically used for application alerts, push e-mails and SMS, and mobile push notifications. A use case for mobile push notifications could be to prompt your inactive users back to using your application again. Targeting mobile platforms for mobile notifications requires integration with different libraries for different platforms. AWS SNS provides a single interface for all these platforms. You send a single push message to SNS, and then SNS sends this message to different platforms, such as the, iOS, Android, and Windows phones.

A topic is the communication channel between publishers and subscribers. Publishers send messages to a topic and subscribers of those messages subscribe to the same topic. Whenever the publisher publishes a message to a topic, AWS SNS delivers the message to all the subscribers of that specific topic.

How to do it...

1. Installing AWS Java SDK.

   In your Maven dependency section, add the following dependency for AWS Java SDK Version 1.9.28.1:

   ```
   <dependency>
       <groupId>com.amazonaws</groupId>
       <artifactId>aws-java-sdk</artifactId>
       <version>1.9.28.1</version>
   </dependency>
   ```

2. Create a topic.

   The following sample program creates a topic called `emailalerts`. Replace endpoint with your own value. Record topic ARN for further usage.

   ```java
   // Create topic.
     public static void CreateTopic() {

       // Create BasicAWSCredentials with Access Key Id
       and Secret Access Key.
       BasicAWSCredentials credentials = new
       BasicAWSCredentials(
               "Access Key Id",
               "Secret Access Key");

       // Create SNS client.
       AmazonSNSClient snsClient = new
       AmazonSNSClient(credentials);

       // Set endpoint.
       snsClient.setEndpoint("sns.ap-southeast-
       1.amazonaws.com");

       // Create topic.
       CreateTopicResult result =
       snsClient.createTopic("emailalerts");

       // Get the topic Arn.
       String topicArn = result.getTopicArn();
   }
   ```

3. Subscribe to a topic.

   In the following sample program, we subscribe to the topic with name `emailalerts` using the e-mail protocol.

```
// Subscribe to a topic.
    public static void Subscribe() {

    // Create BasicAWSCredentials with Access Key Id
    and Secret Access Key.
    BasicAWSCredentials credentials = new
    BasicAWSCredentials(
            "Access Key Id",
            "Secret Access Key");

    // Create SNS client.
    AmazonSNSClient snsClient = new
    AmazonSNSClient(credentials);

    // Set endpoint.
    snsClient.setEndpoint("sns.ap-southeast-
    1.amazonaws.com");

    // Subscribe to a topic by email protocol.
    snsClient.subscribe(
            "arn:aws:sns:ap-southeast-
            1:968336292411:emailalerts", "email",
            "ethan@awscloud.com ");
    }
```

4. Confirm the subscription.

    The user receives a confirmation e-mail from AWS and has to click on the link
    contained in the message.

5. Publish to a topic.

    The following sample program publishes the message to the topic called
    emailalerts:

```
// Publish to a topic.
    public static void Publish() {

    // Create BasicAWSCredentials with Access Key Id
    and Secret Access Key.
    BasicAWSCredentials credentials = new
    BasicAWSCredentials(
            "Access Key Id",
            "Secret Access Key");

    // Create SNS client.
```

```
AmazonSNSClient snsClient = new
AmazonSNSClient(credentials);

// Set endpoint.
snsClient.setEndpoint("sns.ap-southeast-
1.amazonaws.com");

// Publish to a topic.
snsClient.publish(
        "arn:aws:sns:ap-southeast-
        1:968336292411:emailalerts",
        "This is test message.");
}
```

How it works...

First, we install the AWS SDK, as the AWS Java SDK is required to access the AWS services from Java applications.

As AWS SNS topic acts as a communication point for publishers and subscribers to communicate with each other, we first create a topic called `emailalerts`. Copy the ARN topic for use in the subsequent steps.

In the next step, we subscribe an endpoint to our topic. We configure the subscription to send the topic messages to our e-mail address.

At this stage, we receive a confirmation e-mail from AWS. The following screenshot shows a sample confirmation e-mail from AWS:

You have chosen to subscribe to the topic:
arn:aws:sns:ap-southeast-1:968336292411:emailalerts

To confirm this subscription, click or visit the link below (If this was in error no action is necessary):
Confirm subscription

Please do not reply directly to this e-mail. If you wish to remove yourself from receiving all future SNS subscription confirmation requests please send email to sns-opt-out

After the user clicks on the **Confirm subscription** link, he/she will see a subscription confirmed message.

Simple Notification Service

Subscription confirmed!

You have subscribed ~~esbhar@maxbersa.com~~ to the topic: **emailalerts**.

Your subscription's id is:
arn:aws:sns:ap-southeast-1:968336292411:emailalerts:72d8bf97-93de-4410-97e0-63ff5510b2d2

If it was not your intention to subscribe, <u>click here to unsubscribe</u>.

After the confirmation of the subscription, he/she will start getting e-mails from SNS when a new message is published to the topic.

Next, we publish a message to our topic. Here, we publish a message to our e-mail address as defined in a previous step. At this stage, you can access the message in your e-mail application.

There's more...

You can define access control policies to restrict access to specific producers and consumers for a given topic. SNS policies also support cross-account access.

 Each SNS policy must cover only a single topic or queue. Also, each policy must have a unique policy ID, and each statement within the policy must have a unique statement ID.

Amazon SNS also integrates with IAM, so you can specify which SNS-related actions a user is permitted to perform. Hence, you can use IAM policies and/or SNS policies to for setting up your user permissions.

Mobile push notifications are common use case for Amazon SNS. You can send push notifications to mobile devices using one of the supported push notification services. These services include **Apple Push Notification Service** (**APNS**) for iOS, **Google Cloud Messaging** (**GCM**) for Android, and **Microsoft Push Notification Service** (**MPNS**) for Windows Phone.

You can use Amazon SNS with Amazon SQS to store messages to a queue where it can be processed by other application components, asynchronously. You can subscribe a SQS queue to an SNS topic so that when your application publishes a message to the topic, SNS sends an SQS message to the queue.

You can use Amazon SNS to send and receive SMS notifications to mobile phones. A typical use case for this is to send SMS alerts. For example, you can associate a CloudWatch alarm to an SNS topic to send SMS notifications.

In the case of sending notifications to HTTP(S) endpoints, when you publish a notification to the topic, Amazon SNS sends an HTTP POST request to the subscribed endpoint. You have to ensure that your application is ready to handle these HTTP(S) POST requests. Your application should read the HTTP header for messages. There are two key message types that need to be handled—the subscription confirmation and the notifications. For the HTTPS endpoint, you must have a server certificate signed by a trusted **Certificate Authority** (**CA**) that Amazon SNS recognizes.

 Refer to SNS Developers Guide for a list of CAs recognized by Amazon SNS for HTTPS endpoints.

In addition, Amazon SNS is integrated with CloudWatch, so you can collect and analyze metrics for every SNS topic. You can also create alarms and send notifications if the threshold is exceeded for a specific SNS metric, for example, the number of messages failed notifications. API calls to SNS can be tracked via CloudTrail Logs.

Accessing AWS SQS from applications

SQS is a scalable, fast, and fully managed distributed queuing service from AWS. AWS SQS helps you build loosely coupled applications. This allows the application components to run independently with SQS managing the message flow between them. SQS can act as a buffer between the writers and the readers of the messages, and each queue can support multiple writers and readers.

Minimum SQS message size is 1 KB, maximum message size is 256 KB. Messages in SQS queues are stored for 4 days; however, you can increase the retention period from 1 minute to 14 days. You can create an unlimited number of queues, and a queue can contain unlimited number of messages.

AWS SQS supports long polling, so instead of querying SQS every 10 seconds with no results, you can send the request to the SQS. It responds whenever there is a message present in that specific queue.

There is no upfront cost to pay, and you only pay for what you use. Note that due to the distributed nature of the queues, SQS does not guarantee first in, first out delivery of messages.

 If the order of messages is important in your application, then you will need to include sequencing information in your messages and reorder them in the correct order after retrieving them from the queue.

However, SQS does guarantee the delivery of your messages at least once. As AWS SQS stores your messages on multiple servers, it is possible that a message was not deleted on a temporarily unavailable server. This can result in your message being received and processed again. Hence, ensure your application is designed to take care of this situation.

How to do it...

1. Installing AWS Java SDK.

    In your Maven dependency section, add the following dependency for AWS Java SDK Version 1.9.28.1:

    ```
    <dependency>
        <groupId>com.amazonaws</groupId>
        <artifactId>aws-java-sdk</artifactId>
        <version>1.9.28.1</version>
    </dependency>
    ```

2. Creating a queue.

    Execute the following sample program to create a queue called `thumbnailjobinput`:

    ```
    // Create queue.
        public static void CreateQueue() {

            // Create BasicAWSCredentials with Access Key Id
            and Secret Access Key.
            BasicAWSCredentials credentials = new
            BasicAWSCredentials(
                    "Access Key Id",
                    "Secret Access Key");

            // Create SQS client.
            AmazonSQSClient sqsClient = new
            AmazonSQSClient(credentials);

            // Set endpoint.
            sqsClient.setEndpoint("sqs.ap-southeast-
            1.amazonaws.com");

            // Create queue.
            sqsClient.createQueue("thumbnailjobinput");
        }
    ```

3. Insert a message in the queue.

   Execute the following sample program to insert messages into the queue named `thumbnailjobinput`. Here, we are inserting messages with a user ID, and a background thumbnail creation job that monitors this queue, processes the message and creates a thumbnail image for that specific user ID.

```
// Insert message.
public static void InsertMessage() {

    // Create BasicAWSCredentials with Access Key Id
    and Secret Access Key.
    BasicAWSCredentials credentials = new
    BasicAWSCredentials(
            "Access Key Id",
            "Secret Access Key");

    // Create SQS client.
    AmazonSQSClient sqsClient = new
    AmazonSQSClient(credentials);

    // Set endpoint.
    sqsClient.setEndpoint("sqs.ap-southeast-
    1.amazonaws.com");

    // Insert message.
    sqsClient.sendMessage(new
    SendMessageRequest().withQueueUrl(
            "thumbnailjobinput")
            .withMessageBody("123"));

}
```

4. Receive the message in your program.

   Execute the following sample program to retrieve one message at a time from a queue named `thumbnailjobinput`:

```
// Receive message.
public static void ReceiveMessage() {

    // Create BasicAWSCredentials with Access Key Id
    and Secret Access Key.
    BasicAWSCredentials credentials = new
    BasicAWSCredentials(
            "Access Key Id",
            "Secret Access Key");
```

```
// Create SQS client.
AmazonSQSClient sqsClient = new
AmazonSQSClient(credentials);

// Set endpoint.
sqsClient.setEndpoint("sqs.ap-southeast-
1.amazonaws.com");

// Prepare the request.
ReceiveMessageRequest request = new
ReceiveMessageRequest(
        "thumbnailjobinput");

// Set number of messages to retrieve from queue.
request.setMaxNumberOfMessages(1);

// Get messages.
List<Message> lstMessage = sqsClient
        .receiveMessage("thumbnailjobinput")
        .getMessages();

// Iterate through messages.
for (Message message : lstMessage) {

    // Get the message body.
    String msg = message.getBody();
    }
}
```

5. Alternatively, you can also retrieve and delete message from the queue. The following sample program illustrates this:

```
// Receive and Delete message.
    public static void ReceiveAndDeleteMessage() {

    // Create BasicAWSCredentials with Access Key Id
    and Secret Access Key.
    BasicAWSCredentials credentials = new
    BasicAWSCredentials(
            "Access Key Id",
            "Secret Access Key");

    // Create SQS client.
    AmazonSQSClient sqsClient = new
    AmazonSQSClient(credentials);
```

```
        // Set endpoint.
        sqsClient.setEndpoint("sqs.ap-southeast-
        1.amazonaws.com");

        // Prepare the request.
        ReceiveMessageRequest request = new
        ReceiveMessageRequest(
                "thumbnailjobinput");

        // Set number of messages to retrieve from queue.
        request.setMaxNumberOfMessages(1);

        // Get messages.
        List<Message> lstMessage = sqsClient
                .receiveMessage("thumbnailjobinput")
                .getMessages();

        // Iterate through messages.
        for (Message message : lstMessage) {

            // Get the message body.
            String msg = message.getBody();

            // Process the message.

            // Delete the message after processing message.
            String receiptHandle =
            message.getReceiptHandle();

            // Prepare request.
            DeleteMessageRequest deleteRequest = new
            DeleteMessageRequest();

            // Set queue name.
            deleteRequest.setQueueUrl("thumbnailjobinput");

            // Set receipt handle.
            deleteRequest.setReceiptHandle(receiptHandle);

            // Delete message.
            sqsClient.deleteMessage(deleteRequest);
        }
    }
```

How it works...

AWS Java SDK helps you access AWS services from Java applications. You have to create a queue before inserting any data into it. When creating queues, you need to provide unique name for each one of them. SQS assigns each queue a URL that must be used used in all subsequent operations on that queue. SQS returns a message ID for each message in the response to the send message request.

The default polling method for messages is the short or standard polling. In short polling, SQS samples a subset of servers and returns messages from them. Hence, a request need not return all the messages in the distributed queue. If you continue to retrieve the messages, then SQS will sample all the servers and return your messages. SQS also supports long polling which reduces the number of empty responses when the queue is empty. Additionally, in long polling SQS queries all the servers for your messages. We can enable long polling in SQS by setting parameters in `ReceiveMessage`, `CreateQueue`, and `SetQueueAttributes` API calls. In our example, we are using the default polling method, that is, short polling.

While retrieving messages from the queue, you can also specify the number of messages to retrieve. In our example, we specify a value of 1 for the number of messages in our receive message request. Each time a message is received from the queue, you receive a receipt handle with it. This receipt handle is used for deleting the message or changing the message visibility.

 When your processing component receives a message, Amazon SQS does not delete the message, automatically. Hence, your processing component must delete the message from the queue after receiving and processing it.

As the message remains in the queue, SQS blocks it with a visibility timeout, which is the time period during which other processing components in your application cannot receive and process the same message. The default visibility timeout for messages in the queue is 30 seconds, that is, if you don't delete the message after retrieving and processing it within 30 seconds, then SQS makes the message visible again. You can also extend or terminate a message's visibility timeout through the API.

There's more...

SQS provides support for message attributes. These attributes can be used to provide metadata about your message, for example, timestamps. This metadata is useful to processing component to decide on how to process the message without processing the message body.

SQS provides a batch message processing functionality for receiving, sending, and deleting messages, and also for changing the message visibility timeout values. These operations can process 10 messages in a single call. As more work is carried in the batch request, it makes more efficient use of threads and connections; thereby, improving the throughput. Overall costs are also reduced because the number of requests to process the messages is significantly reduced.

Amazon SQS supports dead letter queues. As a best practice, if some messages are not processed successfully, then they should be sent to a dead letter queue. This effectively isolates such messages and avoids repeated processing failures. You can analyze these messages to determine the reason for the processing failures. Dead letter queues should be located in the same region as your other queues.

You can use SQS access policies and/or IAM policies for setting up your access permissions. The main difference between the two is that SQS policies can be used to set up cross-account access to your queues. In addition, Amazon SQS is integrated with CloudWatch, so you can collect and analyze metrics such as the number of empty receives while polling for new messages. You can also create alarms and send notifications if the threshold is exceeded for a specific SQS metric, for example, the number of messages received. API calls to SQS can be tracked via CloudTrail Logs.

8
Deploying AWS Applications

In this chapter, we will cover recipes for:

- ▶ Using Docker containers for AWS deployments
- ▶ Using Chef for AWS deployments
- ▶ Using Puppet for AWS deployments

Introduction

There are several options for deployment, configuration management, and infrastructure management on AWS. These options include Puppet and Chef as configuration management systems, AWS Elastic Beanstalk, AWS OpsWorks, and Ansible as deployment frameworks, and AWS CloudFormation for infrastructure management.

This chapter covers recipes for using open source DevOps tools such as Docker, Chef, and Puppet. Docker implements virtualization and runs both on virtual machines and bare metal. You can directly ship Docker containers to your cloud environments. Chef and Puppet help automate your server and application deployments. These tools treat infrastructure as code, and you can version and test your infrastructure just like any application. These tools will work both on-premise infrastructure and cloud platforms such as Amazon EC2 and OpenStack. In addition, you can use AWS CloudFormation with Chef and Puppet.

 Refer to Wikipedia for more information on DevOps at http://en.wikipedia.org/wiki/DevOps.

Using Docker containers for AWS deployments

Docker containers are like lightweight VMs and allow you to run your application in an isolated environment. Using Docker, you can package your application inside a lightweight container and ship it to your dev, QA, staging, and production environments. Docker's simplified API helps you with the creation and deployment of containers, and its versioning feature helps you easily manage your containers across your environments (that is, dev, test, staging, and production). You can share your Docker images using public registry, Docker hub, maintained by Docker, Inc.

Managing and scheduling these containers in a fleet of machines adds complexity. However, Amazon EC2 Container Service solves this problem for you. Amazon ECS is a container management service that makes it easier to manage Docker containers on an AWS EC2 cluster. This service lets you launch container-enabled application using an API. ECS eliminates the need for your own cluster management and configuration management systems. AWS EC2 Container Service is free to use, you only pay for the resources used. There are open source container orchestration softwares, such as Marathon, that run on top of Apache Mesos, Kubernetes by Google, Docker swarm, and CoreOS fleet.

How to do it...

Installing Docker

The following sample command installs Docker in a Ubuntu 12.04.5 LTS machine:

```
sudo wget -qO- https://get.docker.com/ | sh
```

After installing Docker, verify the Docker version by executing the following command:

```
sudo docker --version
```

Creating a Dockerfile

Create a folder called `myapp` and a file inside that folder called Dockerfile. Our sample Dockerfile contains commands for installing Java and Tomcat.

```
# Specify the base image.
FROM ubuntu:12.04

# Update the local repository.
RUN apt-get update

# Add Java 7 repository.
```

```
RUN apt-get -y install software-properties-common python-
software-properties
RUN add-apt-repository ppa:webupd8team/java
RUN apt-get -y update

# Accept the Oracle Java license.
RUN echo "oracle-java7-installer shared/accepted-oracle-
license-v1-1 boolean true" | debconf-set-selections

# Install Oracle Java.
RUN apt-get -y install oracle-java7-installer

# Install Tomcat7.
RUN apt-get -y install tomcat7
RUN echo "JAVA_HOME=/usr/lib/jvm/java-7-oracle" >>
/etc/default/tomcat7

# Set environment variable.
ENV CATALINA_BASE=/var/lib/tomcat7

# Set entry point.
ENTRYPOINT [ "/usr/share/tomcat7/bin/catalina.sh", "run" ]
```

Building an image from the Dockerfile

By running the following command, you can build an image from Dockerfile. Before executing this command, change the directory to `myapp`.

```
sudo docker build -t sekhar/javatomcat:v1 .
```

You can list the images in your host by running the following command:

```
sudo docker images
```

Creating Docker container

By executing the following command, you can spawn a new container:

```
sudo docker run -d -t -i -p 80:8080 sekhar/javatomcat:v1
```

At this stage, you should be able to browse your web application using the URL `http://host-ip/`.

Checking the container status

Use the following command to list the container ID, image, and ports information:

```
sudo docker ps
```

How it works...

Docker uses resource isolation features of the Linux kernel to sandbox the application, its dependencies, and interfaces in a container. A container can run on any host system having relevant kernel components, while shielding the application from variances of the software installed on any given host. Also, multiple containers can run independently on a single host OS without a hypervisor.

In Docker, images are used to create Docker containers. For example, an image could contain an operating system with Java, Tomcat server, and your web application. You can create these Docker images or use images that other developers created. In this recipe, we used Dockerfile to build images. The Dockerfile is a text document containing a set of commands you would normally execute manually in order to build an image.

The parameters in the Dockerfile are explained as follows:

- ▶ FROM: This is a very important directive in your Dockerfile. It defines the base image to start the build process. You can use previously created images. If an image is not found on the host, Docker will then try to find it in the Docker image index.

- ▶ RUN: Using this directive, you can execute your commands in the build process, for example, installing Java and Tomcat.

- ▶ ENV: Using this directive you, can set up the environment variables. You can access these environment variables in your application inside the container.

- ▶ ENTRYPOINT: You can define your target application using this directive. Whenever a container is created from that image, your application will be the target.

After creating the Dockerfile, we built our Docker image from that Dockerfile. We pass the repository name (sekhar/javatomcat) and tag (v1) for the image. We can use the previously created images to create new containers. You can also spawn as many containers as required from that image.

Finally, we created the Docker container. We specified the host and container port mapping using the -p argument. Here, Tomcat's default port inside container is 8080, so we map the host port 80 to Tomcat port 8080. The -d value indicates that this container will run in detached mode. We also specified the repository name and tag name.

There's more...

Typically, the container is built on the developer's machine. This can make deployments simpler and faster, as it simply involves moving the container to your target environment. In addition, consistency and predictability can be maintained when moving your application code between various environments. The containers can be deployed in AWS environments using AWS Elastic Beanstalk and Amazon ECS.

AWS Beanstalk can deploy your application containers to Amazon ECS. You will need to specify your container images, CPU, memory, ports, and so on. Beanstalk will provision the infrastructure, and place your containers in the cluster and monitor the container's health.

Amazon ECS has been specifically designed to manage containers deployed in a cluster. Amazon ECS provides the cluster management infrastructure and integrates with other AWS services such as ELB, EBS volumes, and IAM. A cluster here is a set of EC2 instances running the Amazon ECS container agent that communicates with the cluster manager and the Docker daemon. The agent registers with the specified cluster and sends EC2 instance and container information. An autoscaling group is associated with the cluster to ensure that the cluster grows appropriately, to meet the container workloads.

 Amazon has developed an ECS-optimized Amazon Linux AMI that includes the ECS agent and the Docker daemon. This AMI is available in the AWS marketplace.

Amazon ECS provides two schedulers—the `RunTask` action (for random distribution of tasks across your cluster) and the service scheduler (for long-running stateless services). The schedulers use the cluster state information from the ECS API to make the placement decisions. Amazon ECS also allow integration of custom and third-party schedulers.

Amazon ECS supports using CloudWatch to monitor the EC2 instances in the cluster. You can view the metrics for Amazon ECS in the ECS and the CloudWatch consoles. The average, minimum, and maximum values for the last 24 hours for cluster CPU and memory and service metrics are available in the ECS console. The CloudWatch console provides a more detailed view of the ECS cluster and service metrics. These metrics include the cluster utilization and service utilization metrics. In addition, you can create CloudWatch alarms. For example, you can create an autoscaling group for the ECS cluster based on cluster memory utilization metric. Amazon ECS is integrated with AWS CloudTrail, so you can use to track the API calls made by Amazon ECS.

Container security can be implemented using AWS IAM, security groups, and VPC configurations. For example, you can create an IAM role and associate it with your container instances (when launch them) so that the ECS container instances calls to ECS and EC2 APIs are authenticated. In addition, you can also leverage Dockers isolation capabilities or use other isolation frameworks such as iptables and SELinux.

Using Chef for AWS deployments

As Chef treats infrastructure as code, you can version control it. Using Chef it's easy to recreate infrastructure again and again. Chef uses a pure Ruby domain-specific language for defining its recipes. Versioning allows you to test your cookbooks before pushing them into the production environment. Resources are the fundamental building blocks of Chef configurations, these represents a piece of the system and its desired state. Resources are gathered into recipes. These recipes are stored in cookbooks.

Chef server holds all the recipes, cookbooks, and policies. You can use a hosted Chef server [by Opscode] or install your own. Chef client on each node download the desired system configuration from the Chef server, and then update the node to comply with the policy.

A node is any physical, virtual, or cloud machine that is configured to be maintained by a Chef client. A Chef role allows us to group configurations for the types of nodes together. Knife is a command-line tool that is used to communicate with Chef server. This is primary tool to create recipes and cookbooks. Chef Knife plugin for EC2 gives knife the ability to create, bootstrap, and manage EC2 instances.

Chef provisioning has an extensible driver system that works with many clouds, virtual machines, containers, and even bare metal. Using the AWS driver, you can work with other AWS resources such as VPCs, S3, and security groups. The drivers available for Microsoft Azure, LXC, Docker, and so on.

How to do it...

Installing the knife-ec2 plugin
In our sample, we will be installing the Chef Development Kit in the `C:\opscode\chefdk` folder. Before executing the following command, change your working directory to `C:\opscode\chefdk\embedded\bin`.

```
gem install knife-ec2
```

Configuring Chef Provisioner node with knife-ec2 plugin
The following sample command creates an Ubuntu machine; hence, we specify the default SSH username to be `ubuntu`. We also specify the AWS access key ID and secret access key. Execute the following command from your workstation:

```
knife ec2 server create
--image "AMI id"
--flavor "t1.micro"
--ssh-key "ProvisionerKeyPair"
--identity-file "ProvisionerKeyPair.pem"
--ssh-user "ubuntu"
--aws-access-key-id "Access Key Id"
--aws-secret-access-key "Secret Access Key"
--region "us-east-1"
```

The preceding command creates an Ubuntu machine in the N. Virginia region. You have to set this client as admin in your Chef server. The following steps show how to set the client as admin from the Chef server web console:

1. Click on the **Clients** option on the top menu from Chef server console.

2. Select the provisioner client (client name is the same as EC2 instance ID) from the client list.

3. Click on the **Edit** option from sub menu.

4. Select the **Admin** checkbox.

5. Click on **Save Client**.

Configuring Chef Provisioner node

You can install the Chef Development Kit using the following command. Execute the following commands as the root user:

1. Download the package using the following command:

   ```
   wget https://opscode-omnibus-packages.s3.amazonaws.com/
   ubuntu/12.04/x86_64/chefdk_0.5.1-1_amd64.deb
   ```

2. After the download completes, run the following command to install the Chef Development Kit:

   ```
   sudo dpkg -i chefdk_0.5.1-1_amd64.deb
   ```

3. Set the Chef driver to `aws`.

   ```
   export CHEF_DRIVER=aws
   ```

4. Create an IAM user with the required EC2 permissions such as permission to launch EC2 instance and generate access credentials for that user. You have to set these credentials in the `~/.aws/config` file. Create the `~/.aws/config` file and add the following lines, replace the access key ID and secret access key with your own AWS credentials:

   ```
   [default]
   output = json
   region = us-east-1
   aws_access_key_id = Access Key ID
   aws_secret_access_key = Secret Access Key
   ```

Creating cookbooks and recipes

In our sample, we provision EC2 instances and then install Nginx server on the EC2 instances.

1. Create a cookbook with name `nginx`. This cookbook has recipes to install Nginx server on EC2 instance.

   ```
   knife cookbook create nginx
   ```

2. Add the resources here to `nginx` cookbook's default [the `default.rb` file] recipe. This recipe downloads the list of available packages, installs `nginx`, starts the `nginx` service, and copies the `index.html` file from the `files/default` subdirectory in the cookbook to the EC2 server's `nginx` folder.

```
execute "apt-get update" do
  command "apt-get update"
end

package 'nginx' do
  action :install
end

service 'nginx' do
  action [ :enable, :start ]
end

cookbook_file "/usr/share/nginx/www/index.html" do
  source "index.html"
  mode "0644"
end
```

3. Add the `index.html` file to the folder specified at this path . . . `/your-chef-repo/cookbooks/nginx/files/default/`.

4. Create cookbook with name `aws_configure`. This cookbook has recipes to provision EC2 instances.

```
knife cookbook create aws_configure
```

5. Add the resources here to the `aws_configure` cookbook's default [the `default.rb` file] recipe. In this recipe, we specify a machine resource called `frontendsrv01`. This EC2 machine will use the image specified in `bootstrap_options`, and the default key/pair generated by Chef client in provisioning node. You can also specify your own key/pair in `bootstrap_options`. In machine resource's, run list we specify the `nginx` recipe.

```
require 'chef/provisioning'

with_machine_options :bootstrap_options => {
  :instance_type => 't1.micro',
  :image_id => 'AMI id'
}

machine 'frontendsrv01' do
    run_list ['nginx']
end
```

6. In the `aws_configure` cookbook's `metadata.rb` file, specify the `nginx` dependency by adding the following line:

```
depends "nginx"
```

7. Upload both cookbooks to Chef server using the following commands:

```
knife cookbook upload nginx
```

```
knife cookbook upload aws_configure
```

Starting Chef client from the provisioning node

After uploading cookbooks, you can run Chef client from the provisioning node. Provide the recipe name when running the `chef-client` command:

```
chef-client -o aws_configure
```

After executing the preceding command, you can see the EC2 instances in your AWS console. These instances are preconfigured with the `nginx` server. You can browse your `index.html` page using `http://EC2 Instance Public DNS/`.

How it works...

The Knife EC2 plugin is distributed as a Ruby gem. First, we install the Knife EC2 plugin and configure the Chef Provisioner node with it. The Chef client in this new EC2 instance adds this node as client to your Chef server. The client name is same as EC2 instance ID.

We assume that you installed Chef server and workstation before proceeding with the recipes. The Provisioner node can be your local workstation machine or a node in cloud. Here, we are bootstrapping an EC2 instance using the Knife EC2 plugin. It installs Chef, and then runs the Chef client with the specified run list. Later, we use this node as Chef Provisioner node. Before executing the command for configuring the Chef Provisioner node, create a key/pair with the name `ProvisionerKeyPair`, download the key/pair into your local machine, and specify the key/pair file path to the following command using the `--identity-file` argument. Chef provisioning is included in the latest Chef Development Kit. We have to install the Chef Development Kit in our Ubuntu machine.

Next, we create and upload our cookbooks and recipes. Finally, we start the Chef client from the provisioning node. Chef provisioning node communicates with AWS to create the EC2 instances.

There's more...

You can use Chef, a configuration management tool, with AWS CloudFormation. This helps avoid manually building a custom AMI and running your own scripts. Instead, you can use Chef to consistently configure and deploy your application. For example, you can use AWS CloudFormation template to provision your web server and database.

After the Amazon EC2 instance is started, AWS CloudFormation installs and configures Chef on the instance. Then, you can use a Chef recipe to configure and deploy your application on the web server. Hence, you can consistently provision the same setup by reusing the CloudFormation template while using Chef to bootstrap your instances. You must have a valid Amazon EC2 key/pair in the region you are launching the template in. In addition, do not hardcode properties that change from stack to stack, or sensitive information (such as passwords), in the template. These can be provided as input parameters in the **Parameters** section of the template.

There are several AWS tools such as AWS OpsWorks and AWS CodeDeploy that help with cloud deployments and software releases. AWS OpsWorks provides a flexible way to create and manage stacks and applications. A stack basically contains Amazon EC2 instances, RDS instances, and many more that need to be managed as a group.

A stack has layers where each layer serves a specific function such as hosting an application server or a database server. AWS OpsWorks includes built-in layers, for example, a stack may include built-in layers for application servers, database servers, load balancers, caches, and so on. AWS OpsWorks uses Chef cookbooks to handle installation and configuration of packages and deployment of applications. It includes a set of built-in cookbooks that support the built-in layers.

A cookbook typically includes attribute files (containing values to be used in recipes and templates), template files (used by recipes to create other files such as configuration files), and recipes (Ruby applications that is required to configure an application—folders, packages, services, and so on). Additionally, you can have a set of recipes assigned to lifecycle events (setup, configure, deploy, underlay, and shutdown). These recipes are executed at the appropriate time. For customization to the layers, you need to override or extend the built-in cookbooks.

AWS CodeDeploy deploys your application code to EC2 instances while ensuring it leaves as many of your instance online as possible. CodeDeploy can also be used in conjunction with Chef recipes.

Using Puppet for AWS deployments

Puppet is an open source platform for provisioning, configuring, and patching applications and OS components. A Puppet deployment has two components: Puppet master and Puppet client. The **Puppet master** is a centralized configuration server that holds the definitions and instructions needed to install your applications. A **Puppet client** connects to the Puppet server and downloads the necessary instructions to install and update the software running on it.

In Puppet, you have to describe machine configurations in Puppet's own **Domain Specific Language** (**DSL**). Central to using Puppet is declaring resources. Each resource describes some aspect of a system, like a file that must be copied or a package that must be installed. Resources are often grouped into classes that are organized into modules. Groups of resource declarations and conditional statements can be specified in a class.

Manifests are files containing Puppet code and are text files saved with a .pp extension. Most manifests are arranged into modules so that they can be automatically located and loaded by the Puppet master. Modules can contain many Puppet classes.

You can find hundreds of modules in the puppet forge website. Puppet comes with a module tool to interact with forge. Geppeto is an Eclipse-based editor for writing Puppet code. Before starting these recipes, you must have a working Puppet master setup with Puppet Version 3.4 or greater and Ruby Version 1.9.

How to do it...

Installing Puppet AWS module in Puppet master

Execute the following steps to install the Puppet AWS module:

1. Install the AWS SDK gem using the following command:

   ```
   gem install aws-sdk-core
   ```

2. Install Retries gem using the following command:

   ```
   gem install retries
   ```

3. Export the AWS access key ID. Replace the AWS access key ID with your own.

   ```
   export AWS_ACCESS_KEY_ID=Access Key Id
   ```

4. Export the AWS secret access key. Replace the AWS secret access key with your own.

   ```
   export AWS_SECRET_ACCESS_KEY=Secret Access Key
   ```

5. Install the Puppet AWS module using the following command:

   ```
   puppet module install puppetlabs-aws
   ```

Launching an EC2 instance with Puppet agent

Execute the following steps in the Puppet master. Our Puppet master is running on an Ubuntu 12.04 LTS machine.

1. Go to the `/etc/puppet/modules` folder.

    1. Create a new module with the name `aws_prod`.

    2. Inside the `aws_prod` module folder, create a new folder called `manifests`.

    3. Inside the `manifests` folder, create a file called `init.pp` with the following content:

```
class aws_prod {

    ec2_instance { 'instance-02':
    ensure          => present,
    key_name        => 'ApacheServerKeyPair',
    region          => 'us-east-1',
    image_id        => 'ami-a6afb8ce',
    instance_type   => 't1.micro',
    user_data       => template('aws_prod/install-agent.sh')
    }

}
```

    The Puppet AWS module allows you to manage AWS using the Puppet DSL. The following code sets up a very basic instance. Here we are passing a shell script that installs Puppet agent in this new EC2 instance.

2. Create a new folder with the name `templates` inside the `aws_prod` module folder.

3. Inside the `templates` folder, create a new file with the name `install-agent.sh`.

4. Add the following content in the `install-agent.sh` file. Replace Puppet server URL with your Puppet server URL.

```
#!/bin/bash
set -e -x
PuppetServer=Puppet Server URL
AgentCertName=$(curl -s http://169.254.169.254/latest/meta-data/
instance-id)
cd ~; wget https://apt.puppetlabs.com/puppetlabs-release-trusty.
deb
dpkg -i puppetlabs-release-trusty.deb
apt-get update
apt-get -y install puppet
echo "
[agent]
```

```
server=$PuppetServer
certname=$AgentCertName
runinterval=5
" >> /etc/puppet/puppet.conf
sed -i /etc/default/puppet -e 's/START=no/START=yes/'
service puppet restart
```

5. You can apply individual manifests using the following command:

   **puppet apply --modulepath=/etc/puppet/modules -e "include aws_
   prod"**

   After executing the preceding command, you can see the new EC2 instance,
   preconfigured with Puppet agent, in the AWS console.

Instead of writing our own module, we can also install the module hosted on the Puppet
Module Forge using the following commands. For example, if we want to install Apache server
on EC2 instance, then execute the following command on Puppet master:

puppet module install puppetlabs-apache

Create a sample `index.html` file in the folder specified at path `/etc/puppet/modules/`
`apache/files`.

In the `/etc/puppet/manifests/site.pp` file add the following content:

```
node 'i-6e3553b8' {

  class { 'apache':
    default_vhost => false
  }
  apache::vhost { 'example.com':
    port    => '80',
    docroot => '/var/www'
  }
  file { '/var/www/index.html':
    source => "puppet:///modules/apache/index.html"
  }

}
```

When the Puppet agent runs, it will install Apache server on your EC2 instance, and you can
browse your `index.html` at `http://EC2 Instance Public DNS/`.

How it works...

Before installing Puppet AWS module, you must install AWS Ruby SDK gem and the Retries gem. If you are using the open source puppet, these gems should be installed into the same Ruby instance used by Puppet. The Puppet module allows you to specify AWS resource types in your manifest files. You can configure AWS resources such as EC2 instances, security groups, VPCs, and so on.

The first time Puppet runs in an agent node, it will send a certificate-signing request to the Puppet master. Before the master is able to communicate and control the agent node, it must sign that particular agent node's certificate. If you want to autosign any new client certificates that are sent to the puppet master, add the following configuration in the [master] section of puppet configuration file (by default, it is located at /etc/puppet/puppet.conf):

```
autosign = true
```

 Do not enable autosigning in your production deployments. Instead of enabling autosigning, you can use basic autosigning or policy-based autosigning.

We also specified the key/pair name, AWS region, image ID, and instance type for our new EC2 instance. When you launch an instance in Amazon EC2, you have the option of passing user data to the instance that can be used to perform common automated configuration tasks and even run scripts after the instance starts.

We created the install-agent.sh file in the templates folder of the aws_prod Puppet module. This shell script gets the instance ID from EC2 instance metadata URL. This is also used for the certificate name, install Puppet agent [Puppet agent Version 3.7.5], and roll out the node with Puppet. The frequency with which the puppet agent applies the catalog is based on the run interval value; here, we have specified it to be 5 minutes (the default value is 30 minutes).

In the case of installing from the Puppet Module Forge, a node statement allows you to assign specific configurations to specific nodes. We specify the previously created EC2 instance ID as the node value and add a virtual host, specify a port, and copy the index.html file from the Apache module to the Apache document root folder.

There's more...

Puppet integrates with AWS CloudFormation. CloudFormation provisions the resources required for your applications. You can use a CloudFormation template to bootstrap a Puppet master. The template specifies the location for content that is used to populate the Puppet master with the application and OS configurations. These configurations can be downloaded to Puppet clients.

AWS CloudFormation also provides a facter plugin that interprets the template metadata to configure applications and roles deployed via Puppet. Using template metadata, you can bootstrap a base OS and the Puppet client, configure roles for the client, and install and run the software packages.

For installing the Puppet client, you can create a template that creates an EC2 instance running the Puppet client (configured to install a server role from the Puppet master). Note that for highly available and scalable applications, you can create multiple instances using an autoscaling group and span across multiple availability zones. You will need to provide the security group and Puppet master DNS name. The Puppet client metadata defines the packages to run, deploy, and configure the client software to access the Puppet master.

AWS CodeDeploy deploys your application code to EC2 instances while ensuring it leaves as many of your instance online as possible. CodeDeploy can also be used in conjunction with Puppet scripts.

Index

A

B

C

D

data services 107
describe-cache-clusters command 123
detailed monitoring 90
DevOps
  URL 155
Docker
  installing 156
Docker containers
  creating 157
  status, checking 157
  using, for AWS deployments 156-159
  working 158
Dockerfile
  creating 156
  image, building from 157
  parameters 158
Domain Specific Language (DSL) 165
DynamoDB
  about 113, 114
  query operation 120
  scan operation 120
  secondary indexes 120
  using 114-120

E

EC2-Classic
  EC2 instance, launching 10
  security groups, creating 20
  used, for launching EC2 instances 9, 10
EC2 instances
  about 2
  adding, to Elastic Load Balancer (ELB) 28
  AMI, creating 34, 35
  AMI, making public 35
  applications, deploying on 62-68
  creating 3-6
  creating, for AWS Marketplace 34
  creating, with multiple NICs 13
  creating, with static private IP address 13
  custom metrics, collecting from 92-97
  EIP, associating to ENI 15
  grouping, placement groups used 24
  launching 3-6launching, in VPC 11
  launching, with EC2-Classic 9, 10
  launching, with EC2-VPC 9, 10
  launching, with Puppet agent 166, 167
  network interface, attaching to 14
  network interface, creating 14
  placing, in placement groups 25
  right storage, selecting 16
  security group, adding 22
  types, selecting 2, 3
  URL 3
EC2 key pair
  about 23
  access, regaining 23
  creating 24
EC2 metrics
  collecting, with CloudWatch 90, 91
EC2-VPC
  security groups, creating 20
  used, for launching EC2 instances 9, 10
ElastiCache
  about 120
  automatic failover, for Redis 124
  user guide, URL 124
  using 120-122
  working 122-124
Elastic IP (EIP) address
  about 12, 38, 67
  allocating 12
Elastic Load Balancer (ELB)
  about 26
  configuring 26
  EC2 instances, adding 28
  health checks, configuring 28
Elastic Network Interface (ENI)
  EIP, associating to 15
e-mail, based on CloudWatch alarm
  sending 100, 101

F

Fn::FindInMap function 60

V

VPC
  about 37
  configuring 38-46
  creating 38-46
  DHCP options, configuring 47, 48
  EC2 instance, launching 11
VPC peering
  configuring 48, 49
VPN
  devices, URL 50
  used, for connecting on-premise
      network to VPC 49-51

W

**Windows Communication Foundation
  (WCF) 80**
Windows/Mac
  AWS CLI, installing with pip 8

Thank you for buying
Amazon EC2 Cookbook

About Packt Publishing

Packt, pronounced 'packed', published its first book, *Mastering phpMyAdmin for Effective MySQL Management*, in April 2004, and subsequently continued to specialize in publishing highly focused books on specific technologies and solutions.

Our books and publications share the experiences of your fellow IT professionals in adapting and customizing today's systems, applications, and frameworks. Our solution-based books give you the knowledge and power to customize the software and technologies you're using to get the job done. Packt books are more specific and less general than the IT books you have seen in the past. Our unique business model allows us to bring you more focused information, giving you more of what you need to know, and less of what you don't.

Packt is a modern yet unique publishing company that focuses on producing quality, cutting-edge books for communities of developers, administrators, and newbies alike. For more information, please visit our website at www.PacktPub.com.

About Packt Enterprise

In 2010, Packt launched two new brands, Packt Enterprise and Packt Open Source, in order to continue its focus on specialization. This book is part of the Packt Enterprise brand, home to books published on enterprise software – software created by major vendors, including (but not limited to) IBM, Microsoft, and Oracle, often for use in other corporations. Its titles will offer information relevant to a range of users of this software, including administrators, developers, architects, and end users.

Writing for Packt

We welcome all inquiries from people who are interested in authoring. Book proposals should be sent to author@packtpub.com. If your book idea is still at an early stage and you would like to discuss it first before writing a formal book proposal, then please contact us; one of our commissioning editors will get in touch with you.

We're not just looking for published authors; if you have strong technical skills but no writing experience, our experienced editors can help you develop a writing career, or simply get some additional reward for your expertise.

Amazon Web Services: Migrating your .NET Enterprise Application

ISBN: 978-1-84968-194-0   Paperback: 336 pages

Evaluate your Cloud requirements and successfully migrate your .NET Enterprise Application to the Amazon Web Services Platform

1. Get to grips with Amazon Web Services from a Microsoft Enterprise .NET viewpoint.

2. Fully understand all of the AWS products including EC2, EBS, and S3.

3. Quickly set up your account and manage application security.

Amazon Web Services: Migrating your .NET Enterprise Application

Evaluate your Cloud requirements and successfully migrate your .NET Enterprise application to the Amazon Web Services Platform

Rob Linton

Amazon SimpleDB Developer Guide

ISBN: 978-1-84719-734-4   Paperback: 252 pages

Scale your application's database on the cloud using Amazon SimpleDB

1. Offload the time, effort, and capital associated with architecting and operating a simple, flexible, and scalable web database.

2. A complete guide that covers everything from installation to advanced features aimed at optimizing your application.

3. Examine SimpleDB and the relational database model and review the Simple DB data model.

Amazon SimpleDB Developer Guide

Scale your application's database on the cloud using Amazon SimpleDB

Prabhakar Chaganti   Rich Helms

Please check **www.PacktPub.com** for information on our titles

Amazon S3 Cookbook

ISBN: 978-1-78528-070-2   Paperback: 280 pages

Over 30 hands-on recipes that will get you up and running with Amazon Simple Storage Service (S3) efficiently

1. Learn how to store, manage, and access your data with AWS SDKs.

2. Study the Amazon S3 pricing model and learn how to calculate costs by simulating practical scenarios.

3. Optimize your Amazon S3 bucket by following step-by-step instructions of how to deliver your content with CloudFront, secure the S3 bucket with IAM, and lower costs with object life cycle management.

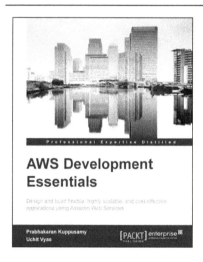

AWS Development Essentials

ISBN: 978-1-78217-361-8   Paperback: 226 pages

Design and build flexible, highly scalable, and cost-effective applications using Amazon Web Services

1. Integrate and use AWS services in an application.

2. Reduce the development time and billing cost using the AWS billing and management console.

3. This is a fast-paced tutorial that will cover application deployment using various tools along with best practices for working with AWS services.

Please check **www.PacktPub.com** for information on our titles